HEALING HIDDEN WOUNDS

A Journey to Liberation

KAREN IBARGUEN

BALBOA.
PRESS

A DIVISION OF HAY HOUSE

Balboa Press books may be ordered through booksellers or by contacting:

Balboa Press
A Division of Hay House
1663 Liberty Drive
Bloomington, IN 47403
www.balboapress.com
1 (877) 407-4847

Because of the dynamic nature of the Internet, any web addresses or links contained in this book may have changed since publication and may no longer be valid. The views expressed in this work are solely those of the author and do not necessarily reflect the views of the publisher, and the publisher hereby disclaims any responsibility for them.

The author of this book does not dispense medical advice or prescribe the use of any technique as a form of treatment for physical, emotional, or medical problems without the advice of a physician, either directly or indirectly. The intent of the author is only to offer information of a general nature to help you in your quest for emotional and spiritual well-being. In the event you use any of the information in this book for yourself, which is your constitutional right, the author and the publisher assume no responsibility for your actions.

Any people depicted in stock imagery provided by Thinkstock are models, and such images are being used for illustrative purposes only. Certain stock imagery © Thinkstock.

Print information available on the last page.

ISBN: 978-1-5043-8869-6 (sc)
ISBN: 978-1-5043-8870-2 (hc)
ISBN: 978-1-5043-8868-9 (e)

Library of Congress Control Number: 2017914621

Balboa Press rev. date: 10/06/2017

PREFACE

With each meditation and prayer that infuses these pages, there is life energy that washes through me. My wish for you, the reader, is that you feel the sacredness within and beyond the words and stories presented here. May you heal as I have healed. May you live your life's purpose, as I live mine.

-Karen Ibarguen

I wrote *Healing Hidden Wounds* in hopes of bringing to light the mental and emotional forces that influence our everyday lives. I especially envisioned that this book would be of benefit to women and men who have experienced some form of trauma in their lives. Be it a singular or repeated exposure to violence, abuse, or other distressing life events, I wanted people to know that human beings are resilient. We can and do heal. The writing of this book, in fact, supported my own life-long process of healing a wound that had been hidden for decades. As I started to write it down and process it in a new way, I developed a deepened awareness of how life itself expanded to meet my needs. When I was ready to heal, doors opened, funds became available, and people came into my life to assist in perfect timing. I experienced first-hand how trust, faith and courage develop with the unfolding of life.

May this book open the hearts of those who are ready to heal or who are currently on the healing path and want to go deeper.

How to Use This Book

Even with faith and the support of my trusted helpers, this book was not easy to write. Parts of it may not be easy to read. Traumas are, by their very nature, traumatic. Talking about them, hearing about them, and reading about them can be difficult to process. For those of you who have experienced trauma, as most of us have, the consideration of traumatic experiences (both our own, and those of others) can bring up memories or wounds that are discomforting, even painful. I made a point to put practices in the book that will help you to feel, sense, and process whatever emotions, feelings or sensations may arise.

Those of you who are new to processes of self-healing may want to go directly to chapter six to engage in a few mindfulness exercises before beginning the book. Many people find that such practices enable them to *be* with their thoughts and emotions in a neutral way. We can practice how to accept what is and act consciously, rather than reacting to the mental dramas that tend to accompany emotions and embodied experiences. Each practice can be a stand-alone exercise or can be done in succession. I recommend that you practice each of them at least once so that you can find the ones that help you to feel at ease and speak to you the most.

As you read *Healing Hidden Wounds*, know that you can return to chapter six for help in processing any feelings, emotions, or sensations that may arise. Just take a few moments to bookmark your page and skip to the exercises. After you feel settled, pick up where you left off.

If you have experienced trauma in your life and have not undergone more traditional psychological therapy, I highly recommend that you build a relationship with a therapist or counselor. Ask for a referral from a trusted friend or family member. Ask the therapist questions before you decide to work with that person. You have the right to be sufficiently informed of their expertise and therapeutic approach. The qualities to look for and expect are: honesty, awareness, compassion, courage, and openness.

As you make your way through the pages of this book, you'll travel with me to the far reaches of the world, walk with me up high peaks, and sit with me in meditation. You'll also hear about my own traumatic experiences and consider what happens when traumas remain hidden. For those already on the healing path, I recommend having an empathetic witness available, or with you, as you read the heavier chapters. Two chapters (1 and 4) may bring up feelings stemming from known traumas or those that have been unconsciously hidden. That is what happened to me.

When a long-held trauma surfaced unexpectedly, I was fortunate that my friend and energy worker, Eva, held the space for me. Her being with me, calm and without judgement, allowed my emotions to play out fully as they arose. She understood and supported me as I needed. In fact, Eva is also an *enlightened witness*, one who has done the work on her own childhood traumas and has learned to find love and compassion for her inner child. She helped me to realize and trust that one can experience trauma in life and still fulfill one's purpose.

For inspirational speaking, trainings and workshops go to www.karenibarguen.com.

ACKNOWLEDGEMENTS

Many thanks to Gayle Sulik, Ph.D. for your extraordinary editorial and linguistic skills, bringing this book to life. This book would not be the same without your tireless dedication to pulling out the full story for the readers as well as for my own healing. A deep bow of gratitude.

There are no words to thank you Eva Hunter; my friend, energy worker and world traveling sister. My deepest gratitude for your encouragement, support and clear feedback each step of the way in the evolution of this book as well as my healing. You are a gift.

I offer my gratitude to all of the Gurus I have met in everyday or unexpected places. And to the sacred teachings across many religions and systems of ancient knowledge in the U.S. and around the world.

From the bottom of my heart, I thank you all!

TABLE OF CONTENTS

TO THE LIGHT

The sparkling golden cocoon surrounds and protects me
while nourishing and sustaining perfect energy
for my metamorphosis from larvae to moth.

I surrender my beliefs
of how life should be.
The alchemy of life unfolds unto me.

Knowing now my eternal Self,
the moth flies into the flame
and no thing remains.

Photo by Warren Photographic

Chapter 1

A SOMATIC IMPRINT OF TRAUMA

There has been a revolution in how we perceive the body. What appears to be an object, a three-dimensional anatomic structure, is actually a process, a constant flow of energy and information.

-- Deepak Chopra, Co-Founder, The Chopra Center [1]

The body is more than flesh and blood. It is a complex system that does everything from organize your thoughts and direct your gait, to affect your mood and regulate your daily constitution. Modern science can directly measure many types of energetic charges in the body. What cannot be measured directly are the subtle energies: those of emotions, feelings, intelligence and wisdom.

Stuart Zoll describes a complex communication system linking one's psychic and somatic experiences. [2] Subtle energy centers in the body called chakras send signals between the emotional, mental, and spiritual realms. These transformative centers connect with an energy highway called the acupuncture meridian system to access every part of the body. Chakras also hold the resonance of memories and emotions at a cellular level.

For thousands of years, energy workers and healers have harnessed the body's subtle energies for curative purposes. Acupuncture, Reiki, Reflexology, Yoga, breath work, and many other practices involve practitioners who sense and direct the flow of the subtle energies of the body. Since memory patterns and somatic experiences have the capacity to change cellular structure and functioning, at times leading to chronic disease and disorder,[3] such techniques can release blocked energy to induce a natural healing response.

Feeling Energy in the Body

> Emotions ...play out in the theater of the body.
> Feelings play out in the theater of the mind.
>
> -- Antonio Domasio, *Descartes' Error:*
> *Emotion, Reason, and the Human Brain.*[4]

I'd like to share a life-changing energy session I had with my friend Eva, an energy worker who helped me to unearth and begin to heal a deep emotional wound.

We started the session in the usual way. After having a cup of tea together, we go to the treatment room. I take off my shoes and jewelry and lie face up on a massage table. Eva covers me with a blanket. She centers herself to calm her mind, slow her breathing, and "ground" her physical state. Passing her hands slowly above the surface of my body to scan my energy field, she gets a sense of energetic imbalances that manifest as heat, cold, pressure, heaviness, lightness, or other sensations. She asks me to do a mental scan of my body to notice any sensations for myself.

I take a deep breath and mentally scan my body from my feet upwards. I wiggle my toes, squeeze my calf muscles and thighs. My legs soften as soon as I stop the contractions. I squeeze and relax my hands, then my arms. It feels good to feel tension leaving my body. My breathing slows, and each breath is softer and longer. My mind quiets. I feel the weight of my head on the pillow, sense my scalp, and notice that I am clenching my jaw. I relax my face, separating my back rows of teeth. I pay attention to each area of my body, take a slow breath and exhale. Progressively, each area softens.

I arrive at my chest and belly, where I detect a feeling of heaviness in my lower right abdomen. At this point, something extraordinary begins to happen that will change my body and how I view myself in the world.

I tell Eva about the dense feeling in my gut. She asks, "Does it have a size, shape, texture, color, or other discernible features?"

"Yes. It's a small rectangle along my hip crease where my leg and abdomen join. It's smooth and thick, with a brownish color. Very heavy."

Eva places one of her hands on my shoulder, the other on my opposite hip. She presses outward to stretch and lengthen both sides. She rocks my hips back and forth gently for several minutes. The heaviness dissipates. Suddenly, I experience myself as a little girl and start to cry.

In my vision, or whatever it is, my five-year-old body is bent in half. Little Karen rolls up like a ragdoll and flutters open her eyes. Everything is bright. Slow blinks soften the glare. She's been face down for so long; she needs to get her bearings. She scans to the right and left, then stretches her nimble fingers to the sky. There she is in her pink dress with the straps across the top and that short-sleeved white shirt. Donning her favorite black patent leather shoes to make the outfit just so, she skips next door to her backyard. There's the sandbox!

I step out of my quasi-dreamlike state for a moment to realize that this little girl truly is me. I'm not just watching her on the screen of my mind. I am experiencing exactly what she's experiencing in her own body, which is my body. Consciousness shifts again, and five-year-old me tells Eva that she wants to go play in the sand.

Committed to taking this experience wherever it needs to go, Eva asks if I want to take my shoes off. "No. I want to play with my shoes on." I scamper to the sandbox, a happy kid.

After a short while I get the urge to go inside my house. There I go, running straight through the back door to find the whole family in the living room; Dad, brothers, and sister wrestling on the floor and Mom on the couch as usual laughing at the commotion. I can't resist the rumpus. I dive onto the floor to roll around with my clan. I play with Mom, too. It's a great reunion!

I abruptly become aware of Eva. "What just happened? Was

I transported to another dimension? Was I hallucinating? I'm pretty sure my body never left the therapy room."

Eva told me that energy work has a strong emotional component. When she helped me to break up that heavy, brown energy blockage it facilitated an emotional release from the embodied memory of a five-year-old girl. This made sense to me. My next-door neighbor sexually assaulted me in his back yard when I was five years old. That memory was tucked away in the lower right quadrant of my abdomen for 50 years.

Unlocking Memory: The Boy Next Door

I'll call him Johnny. He was about 16 years old. If I looked out the front window of our living room, his house was on the left. It was eternally dark, with curtains tightly closed. Johnny's mother made miniature clothes for my sister's Barbie doll. She went over more often than me to pick up the latest fashions. Nothing seemed out of the ordinary. Not that we knew of.

One day when my sister asked five-year-old me to pick up Barbie's weekly wardrobe, I ended up in the garage with Johnny. He called me over just as I was about to scoot next door. Standing at his father's tool bench, attentive and smiley, he asked to see the doll clothes. I displayed his mother's handiwork. Johnny stood next to me and rubbed my back. I liked back rubs. Sometimes I'd curl up in my mom's lap on the couch and fall asleep as she caressed me. Johnny's fingers wandered from my back to my arms and legs, and then graced my nipples. That startled me. He didn't linger there long enough for his touch to register as anything more unusual than the rest of this impromptu 'massage.' Besides, I was anxious to deliver Barbie's latest swag. I stashed the clothes back in the bag and darted home. My sister dressed Barbie with lightning speed as I awaited the evening fashion show. I didn't give Johnny or the garage scene a second thought.

Later that year, Johnny did something much worse.

I was playing in my neighbor's backyard like I'd done many times before when Johnny asked me to go to the playhouse. I'd never been inside the make-shift shed for children. I mostly forgot it was there. Submerged in overgrown brush on the other side of his property, the dank shack blended in with a woody background that almost screamed 'keep out.' As soon as we entered the one-room structure, Johnny closed the door behind us. I didn't even have time to look around before he pushed my head down into his crotch. "Bite down," he ordered. Confused, I tried to do what I was told. The zipper of his Levis scratched my lip.

Johnny grabbed my hand, pulled me back out the door we went in, and dragged me over to the bushes on the far side of the shack. I tripped over roots and overgrown brush until I lost my balance and fell to the ground. I remember him pulling my pants down as he pressed me close, his clammy hand holding my mouth shut. I couldn't breathe. My arms didn't move. Time slowed down until it almost stopped. I froze. I left my body, dissociated with no understanding of what was happening to me. I didn't know until decades later that Johnny raped me.

When Johnny finished handling me, he backed away and told me NOT to tell anybody what happened. I nodded, pulled my pants up, and ran full speed to my house. My clothes were filthy from the dirt and brush, and from what I now know was semen. I threw the sticky mess into the hamper. I don't know what I did after that. I was outside my body, delirious.

A few days later I felt pain and burning when I peed. Sure enough, this little five-year-old developed something rare for girls her age, a severe bladder infection. My parents noticed right away and took me to the doctor. The infection was bad. I had to be admitted for exploratory surgery. I remember the anesthesia. I tried to push the mask away, to escape, to breathe. Then suddenly. I was *awake*. It was over. They discharged me after a few days with a catheter, some antibiotics, and other small pills. I have no memory of how I felt physically or emotionally after I got home.

The doctor-in-charge asked my parents to monitor my urine output for a day or two and then recommended that the catheter be removed. It was 1961. I'm not sure why this removal procedure happened at home instead of in the doctor's office. At any rate, my dad stood at the left side of my bed to cut the catheter so that the small balloon inside my bladder would collapse and the catheter could be pulled out. It didn't feel good. I could tell that my dad felt awkward. The worried look on my mother's face told me that she didn't want to be the one to do this to me either. I knew he wasn't trying to hurt me or do anything bad. Still, I had a shameful sense that my privacy was being violated, by my dad.

I went back to the doctor for urine tests every month for six months. Each time, my mom held my hand as they put in another catheter to get yet another urine sample, a "clean catch" as they say, to evaluate the color and look for blood. It was painful, and I felt degraded every time. I never blamed Johnny for any of it. In my child's naivety, I didn't relate the backyard incident to being sick 'down there.' I didn't tell anybody what happened that day – not my parents, not my family, not my friends. I put it out of my head. I did have a generalized feeling of fear after that though, and a sense that life isn't fair. I never did return to that yard.

During the initial office visit my father asked the doctor point blank how his little girl could have gotten such an intense urinary tract infection. "Could it have been the result of sexual assault?" The doctor said he couldn't make a definitive conclusion nor could he rule it out. I had no other risk factors or underlying conditions to explain the intensity of the infection.

My parents didn't probe further, and they never knew for sure. And they never asked me any questions about sexual activity or inappropriate behavior. Maybe they felt guilty for not being able to protect their child. Then again, awareness of childhood sexual abuse was more limited back then and therapy for children was not common.

Nobody knew about Johnny's abusive behavior or suspected him of anything sinister. Why would they? There was a societal denial surrounding sexual assault. Even today, the vast majority of people do not want to believe how prevalent it is. It's far easier to shut down and ignore such an overwhelming reality. Besides, Johnny was friendly, did his chores, never vandalized the neighborhood. People liked him. He was a good kid. Except that he molested little children. I wasn't the only one. Eventually he was found out, and found guilty.

Growing Up in my Own Little World

The sexual assault of five-year-old Karen was bottled-up for many years. As I look back, I see how much energy it took for me to repress that traumatic experience. As far as I could remember I had a fun and fulfilling childhood, the love of two parents, two brothers, and a sister. I had a sense of security.

We lived in a small house in a south Texas suburb, until I was nine years old. After that my parents built a home a few miles away, which put a comfortable distance between Johnny and me. We were a family who loved sports. Both of my brothers played baseball from childhood to college and were drafted into the major leagues: The New York Mets and St. Louis Cardinals. I was an avid softball player myself and earned a scholarship to a large state university. I had the outward trappings of happiness and good social adjustment: the grim reality was that I was lost, shy, and unable to connect with people.

It wasn't until my thirties, around 1989, that the early abuse started to surface. Many of the details remain fuzzy. After I made sense of it enough to explain it to someone, I disclosed the incident to my younger brother and his wife. I said, in so many words, that I was sexually assaulted by the boy next door when I was five. They were shocked. They listened with concern and empathy, assuring me that they would do anything I asked or needed. They were the first family members I told.

Speaking that truth was good for me. It empowered me to acknowledge two other sexual assaults I experienced as a teenager. While I did not repress those other traumas, I didn't tell anyone about them either, not for a very long time. I'd learned to be silent in the face of trauma.

It's Happening Again

When I was 14 years old, a man entered my house and raped me. He was not a stranger or someone unreliable. I knew and trusted him. So did my family. One day when no one else was home, he made his way to my bedroom while I was doing homework. He flung himself on top of me, knocking my books to the floor. I froze, just like when I was 5 years old—retreating to that space of inner numbness, unable to defend myself and unaware of what I needed to resist that kind of force. When he was done, I ran to the bathroom to wash myself clean. He retreated as I soaked in the bathtub, angry and defiant behind a locked door.

I was old enough to hate what had happened to me, to feel belligerent about being violated, and so violently. It never occurred to me that I could tell anyone about what happened. For one, it was embarrassing and shameful. Even though I wanted to push this guy off of me and defend myself, I couldn't. I froze, helpless and unable to make a sound. The physical and emotional pain from when I was a breathless little girl forced into the dirt beneath the weight of a boy three times my age worked in conjunction with the terror lurking beneath Johnny's menacing threat 'not to tell.' That wound was deeply imprinted in my psyche, and in my body.

I did my best to separate myself from the rape. When I was in high school it almost happened again when a guy from one of my classes asked me out. He had a cute smile and was nice to me. I didn't know him very well. I thought we might have enough in common to go out and have a good time. He sweetened the invitation with an offer to drive me around in his new fiery red convertible. I loved that car!

He picked me up on a Friday night, and we zoomed around town for hours with the top down, my hair whipping around in the wind. I felt alive and unencumbered. At a stoplight, he reached over to drop a little blue pill into the palm my hand. "It'll make you feel good," he said in a lyrical tone. I didn't think anything of it. I'd experimented with recreational drugs before. Many kids at school did. I took a sip of Coke to wash it down.

A while later he drove into a park where some of the kids from school hung out. I'd seen them around though didn't know their names. We'd only talked to them for a few minutes before he said, "Let's go." We hopped back into the car. I wondered where we were headed next.

We proceeded slowly around the park until we reached a secluded area near some trees. He pulled over and turned off the engine. Without a word, he got out of the car and opened the trunk. Presenting me with a plaid wool blanket as if it were a gift from the magi, he smiled and motioned me to join him. I pressed the door handle to get out of the car. I was already loopy from that little pill. He helped me out of my seat and escorted me over to a grassy patch beyond the trees. After he unfolded the blanket to a perfect square, he plopped down, patting the spot next to him. Our eyes met. My noodly legs wilted as I planted myself alongside my new friend.

With a tree trunk as place to rest my back, I settled into my seat on the ground. I felt good. I was happy. Calm. Before I could take a breath, my companion burrowed into my personal space like a black-tailed prairie dog. Before I knew it, my pants were down. I couldn't move. I had no interest in being part of this rodent's coterie, but I wasn't in any shape to hold my ground. The drugs kicked in. I could barely see straight.

Lucky for me, some recreational drugs cause more than dizziness and blurred vision. He couldn't get an erection. Exasperated at his misfortune, my suitor gave up. "Let's go. I'll take you home." I barely got my pants zipped up before he was pulling me up from our makeshift bedchamber. He helped me into the car and slammed the door. He couldn't get me home fast enough. He dropped me off and sped away.

I blundered along the front sidewalk to the door, maintaining enough composure to walk straight to my room without talking to anyone. Luckily, the staircase was right inside the front door, so I could walk by unnoticed. I plunked down onto my bed and slept until the next morning. The convertible guy's idea of a good time was much different from mine. His needs were the only part of the equation.

We passed each other in the hall at school that following Monday without exchanging a glance. We maneuvered around each other like water gushing around rocks in a stream. Unlike water doing what it does naturally to fulfill its purpose, I was not an active presence in this world. With self-realization stripped away, I was invisible. I had no personal power to confront my attacker. Not this one; not the others. I told no one. This predator's vicious power over me tunneled into my consciousness. I didn't even go to my graduation. My parents never knew why, and they never pushed me to go.

A Pathway to the Heart

I thought I'd come to terms with the sexual assaults of my youth, processed them as they say in therapy circles. Meanwhile the trauma that began with five-year-old Karen's rape was energetically fixed into the lower right quadrant of my abdomen—a domicile of remembrance, and pain. The only place my inner child could feel happy and safe was in that sand box. That's where she stayed for a long, long time.

That day with Eva the energy work triggered the start of a profound healing process. I cried from the depths of my belly and felt such lightness of being after that session. Eva told me I could call on my little girl any time. I could communicate with my young self, forge an inner relationship with her while allowing whatever feelings or sensations that arise to occur without judgment or story. Just a willingness to experience my somatic self. Doing this has helped me to come to terms with the assaults and to free up other energy blockages in my body. Having said that, I understand that the true capacity to heal deep wounds comes from the power to go inward. The remainder

Chapter 2

THE JOURNEY BEGINS

A psychic told me once, "You're like this beautiful picture on the wall that no one can touch." The comment echoed a conversation I'd overheard years earlier from a friend who uttered, a bit too loudly, "I've known Karen for years, but I don't *really* know her." I didn't understand at the time how I could be such a mystery. We spent years having dinners together, going hiking and biking, meeting up with friends. I guess the psychic was right.

I understand in retrospect that my childhood trauma kept me inaccessible for much of my life. I wasn't able to connect on a deeper level, even with people I cared about greatly. I protected myself, hid my vulnerability. I know that traumatic experiences can lead to self-imposed isolation to help people to feel safe and secure. Unfortunately, without developing ways to deal with the resultant emotional and behavioral reactions, those experiences can live on in a one's deepest memories, embodied experiences, and interpersonal relationships. Despite my insight into the role trauma has played in my life, I didn't know how to change my situation.

After a time, giving meaning to my childhood wounds became a kind of quest that would help me to move on with my life in a holistic way. Healers, gurus, and friends came along at the right moments to help me to expand my self-inquiry and connect with *something higher*. I finally got to a point where I could listen to my inner voice and say, "Yes, I am ready to heal." That moment was the start of something new: an integration of mind, body, and spirit.

One of my first spiritual guides was a Reiki healer I met in 2006. Reiki is a spiritual healing technique of Japanese origin that makes reference to the spirit of a higher power (i.e., God's wisdom). The term literally unites the universal (rei) and life force energy (ki). The philosophy behind reiki centers on energy flow. Strong, fluid energy in the body promotes vitality whereas weak, stagnant or blocked energy can contribute to physical symptoms or emotional imbalances. Reiki practitioners use hand positions on or above the body to move and balance vital energy.

With attention and practice, anyone has the capacity to feel, focus on, and guide the energy in and around the body. For this reason, Reiki is especially accessible to those who engage in mind-body practices such as yoga, tai chi, or meditation. I was a perfect candidate for learning the technique from my teacher.

During one of our sessions, she told me about an energy system called Merkaba (also spelled Merkabah), which is an early form of Jewish mysticism that involves Divine light as a vehicle of ascension. Mer (light)-Ka (spirit)-Ba (body) refers to the spirit/

body surrounded by rotating fields of light pivoting at the heart center. I didn't fully grasp the philosophy. After learning more, I incorporated the practice into my daily meditation. I'd sit silently and take several slow, long breaths. I'd hold my breath after each exhalation, just for a few seconds. It wouldn't take long until I'd feel still and centered, as if my body balanced itself effortlessly, barely needing any muscular energy to hold the position I was in. At this point I'd imagine two pyramids of energy, one pointing up from the ground toward the crown of my head, the other starting just above my head and pointing down to the ground. A subtle sensation of energy would develop from where these two forces overlapped. I'd visualize the lower pyramid spinning to the left, the upper spinning to the right.

Whenever I used the Merkaba technique, I'd become aware of the energy in and around my body. A stirring in my belly would accelerate steadily, expanding outward from my physical being, sometimes beyond the room or the house. I'd feel light, at times weightless, with a sense of peace and contentment. I liked the practice. Nevertheless, it didn't cultivate the deep joy and expansion I longed for, what I now think of as *a centering in my heart that reaches toward higher consciousness.*

As I persisted on my spiritual path, I found a website for The School of Remembering, a training program that builds on ancient, sacred knowledge to help people to live in a harmonic, loving, compassionate, joyful, and abundant way. The school's creator, Drunvalo Melchizedek, is an author and visionary healer who translated this knowledge into modern concepts that are accessible to seekers like me. Melchizedek explains,

> When the Mer-Ka-Ba is directly connected to
> the Sacred Space of the Heart, that person's life
> becomes interconnected to all life everywhere
> and moves into higher consciousness naturally.[5]

These teachings expand upon the heart centering and Merkaba practices I'd been using to try to access something beyond my immediate human experiences. I immediately called to register for a retreat in Sedona, Arizona called "Awakening the Illuminated Heart."

The registrar told me that the event was already full but that a space might open up. I optimistically booked a flight. Alas, the power of positive thinking did *not* get me a spot. An email notification confirmed that the retreat was at capacity. Disappointment soon gave way to musing about nature and exploration. Why not take this opportunity to venture to an energizing land of hiking trails, red rock canyons, and scenic byways? It was an easy sell. I already had a prepaid airline ticket.

As the expiration date on my flight to Sedona closed in, I started to research the goings-on for that time of year. July and August are monsoon season; hiking plans could be derailed. A conference called the *Dawn of a New Time* (2012) intrigued me. An assembly of indigenous elders from the Sierra Nevada of Santa Marta, Colombia in South America, the Arhuacos and Kogi Mayans, was gathering in Sedona to share ancient wisdom with their younger brothers (i.e., Western civilizations) about safeguarding what they call *the seed of life* – or, the relationship between human beings, the earth, and the universe. I signed up.

An Ancient Tribe with an Urgent Warning

To give some background, the Kogi Mayans are an isolated, fully intact civilization, free from outside intrusion for most of its existence. The tribe fled to a remote mountain in the Sierra Nevada de Santa Marta, Colombia when the Spanish invaded the Americas 500 years ago. Quite literally running for the hills. The Kogi have sustainably cultivated this part of the world for thousands of years. Grounded in a belief that the earth is a living being, they see *damage to any part as damage to the whole.* Tending to the planet with care is their reason for all existence.

In 1990, a BBC documentary by Alan Ereira introduced this remote tribe to the western world to share a serious existential message and urgent admonition about the dangers of environmental degradation. The Kogi warned that damage to the environment put the world on a path toward catastrophic devastation. Incidentally, a wealth of scientific evidence supports this fact. Tampering with the environment to mine resources, build power stations, and construct infrastructures to support modern living has already had multiple, large-scale impacts on local and global ecosystems. Twenty-three years after the Kogi's initial cinematic call to action, they saw too little conservation or remediation to have a significant impact.

In a second plea to the western world, the tribe called BBC filmmaker Ereira back to their home to create another film, entitled *Aluna*. The principle of Aluna refers to a universal consciousness that is the source of all life and intelligence.[6] Ereira explains more about this indigenous life code in an interview with *The Guardian:*[7]

> Aluna is something that is thinking and has self-knowledge. It's self-aware and alive. All indigenous people believe this, historically. It's absolutely universal. Aluna needs the human mind to participate in the world – because the thing about a human mind is that it's with a body. Communicating with the cosmic mind is what a human being's job is as far as the Kogi are concerned.

In other words, the Kogi tradition of environmental stewardship originates from *enlightenment*: spirit and environment are inseparable.

Aluna is central to the Kogi belief system. In fact, certain members of the tribe are raised in darkness during their early years to learn to cultivate an inner awareness that allows them to connect with cosmic consciousness, respond to its needs, and keep the world in balance. These are the Kogi Mamos (meaning, spiritual leaders or enlightened ones) who seek to communicate interconnections in the natural world. By coming out of hiding through film and assembly, the Kogi hope to raise awareness of the existence and value of theirs and similar tribes around the world in saving the planet from the spiritual and environmental damage of modernization.

Witnessing the Dawn of a New Time

As the end of June (2012) rolled around, I prepared myself to meet the Kogi at their two-day *Dawn of a New Time* conference. Anxious to hear the Mayan elders share their message about how to live in harmony with the Earth and restore the natural order, I'd be part of an important cultural exchange. The elders would address international spiritual leaders and registered participants in a series of moderated sessions (translated into English for the audience) on possible solutions to an environmental and spiritual crisis. Also, we'd bear witness to prayers, blessings, music, and ancient teachings.

The formal program was not at all what I expected. The sessions were intense and almost impossible for me to follow. Listening to a language that is not your own is challenging enough, because emotions and passionate exchanges can easily get lost in translation. The four elders involved, well, they are quite impassioned about their message. All I was getting were the words, and sometimes not even those because lag time from speech to interpretation made it worse. In my frustration, I could feel my heart pounding faster and faster. I think I stopped breathing at one point. I respect the elders immensely and value what they have to say. Still, I couldn't wait to get out of there. The next day I slept in and skipped the morning session. Some leisurely sightseeing held more appeal than another three hours of confusing banter.

By the time I got to the afternoon session, the closing ceremony had already ended. I arrived just in time to see the

Mamos getting ready to load onto a bus. I was introduced to each of them, and we hugged goodbye. One of the men embraced me with such powerful resonance it was as though love itself emanated from my heart in all directions. I dwelled on that *expanded heart sensation* for hours as I drove around town, ate my dinner, and lingered in my hotel, fully present and content. I was calm and centered. I wanted to know more about that powerful feeling. Was it transmitted to me, or merely recognition of my own eternal truth? I knew in an instant that I'd meet the Kogi again, this time in their homeland.

A Time for Contemplation

I stayed in Sedona three days after the conference ended to explore the area's well known spiritual vortexes. These energy centers are located throughout the region and contain documented levels of natural electromagnetic earth energy.[8] People can feel the calming or invigorating effects. Some of the sites are more magnetic (i.e., yin, from the Taoist philosophy of duality and referencing the dark/lunar/night/feminine/ intuitive side of life). These are places to practice inner work like meditation and contemplation. Others are more energizing (i.e., yang, representing the Taoist concepts of light/solar/day/ masculine/aggressive). Visitors say that these locations bring about feelings of stamina and vigor. Other sites are more balanced (both yin and yang) and offer clarity and higher vision.

The magnetic vortex I was drawn to is a well-known natural cathedral called Cathedral Rock. It's one of the most photographed red rock formations in Sedona, colloquially called "the womb with a view." Known for its feminine energy, people who go there say it evokes compassion, patience, empathy, and peace. I woke up on a Monday morning ecstatic to hike in a place with such magnetic, nurturing energy.

When I first laid eyes on Cathedral Rock I was overcome by its sheer scale and majesty. I had to take a moment to let it soak in. I sat down on the ground, closed my eyes and meditated. The energy in my body magnified, as if to join with the sacred formation. My mind settled, and I had a profound sense of peace. When I opened my eyes to the mountain's brilliance, a smile crept onto my face. I sat in a state of bliss, in awe of nature and my place in it.

Cathedral Rock; Sedona, Arizona
Photo by Scott McAllister, Art Collections

I hiked to the top of the rock formation to meet a baby blue sky blotted with cotton ball clouds. Expanses of red rock strata stretched for miles. I walked on, hour by hour. When I got to the end of the trail I sat down to meditate again. Endless moments passed. A low-pitched growl erupted from my gut to remind me to recharge my physical reserves. I crunched into a crisp Gala apple and chewed deliberately, savoring the juicy splendor all around me. With sated belly and soul, I was ready to ease back down the Cathedral's steep decline. By the time I reached the trail base, my knees wobbled between rock hard calves and taut hamstrings. Just a short drive and I'd be tenderizing them in an Epsom salt bath.

I slept hard that night and didn't worry about being the early bird the next morning. I was tired from hiking. More so, it takes time and energy to integrate one's experiences. I was bursting from meeting the Kogi and from many hours of meditation. I needed rest.

After a laid-back morning, I went to another site with a vortex, the Bell Rock formation.[9] This hike has several paths to the top. Overall, it's a more challenging hike than I'm used to. One of the trails is exceptionally narrow and isolated, with a sharp climb and cliffs at the edges. Treacherous for inexperienced hikers, I wanted to avoid it. I started out on one of the easiest, most popular trails. About half way up, I turned around as I prefer paths less traveled.

Bell Rock; Sedona Arizona
Photo by Scott McAllister, Art Collections

I came to a more tapered trail where two people were leaving. From the map, it looked like a longer walk. The sunsets from the peak were supposed to be well worth the effort. Besides, I had plenty of stamina. The hike seemed effortless. Bell Rock is known for its stimulating yang energy. I was good to go.

The first hour on the trail was easygoing, with no hikers to distract me from a mindful passage. Then without warning, the trail constricted to a thin line etched into a vertical cliff. Rocks tumbled from an escarpment above onto the gravelly path in front of me before spilling down the steep precipice that hugged the path. I stopped in my dusty tracks, momentarily breathless. My body congealed as my once steady breath converted to a reedy pant. I was alone on a perilous, secluded trail. If I were to slide off the cliff, no one would know. I might not survive. I stared at the path ahead of me. The landscape went on as far as I could see. My heart raced in fear. I had to settle down.

The irony of facing existential reality while on a quest for self-inquiry was not lost on me. Any animal, including humans, will fight, flee or freeze in the face of actual danger. Crafting a story about one's demise on the lone cliffs of Sedona, that's different. That kind of fear is a mind trap wrought out of history and social conditioning. I'm not making an argument for reckless endangerment: We all need to confront our fears to live more fully and make skillful decisions. Fear of death is the biggie. In that moment of clarity, I deepened my breath and made a sound decision: I would not, as I'd planned, be looking out from Bell Rock's peak at sunset. I turned around and stumbled the rocky pathway back toward the trailhead. The slim line of dirt returned to a wide, hard surface. I bowed my heavy head in gratitude.

Under normal circumstances, the relief of steady conditions would have put my mortal fears to rest. Nonetheless the image of my body plummeting to the depths of a stony grave haunted me with every step. If my desire to connect with something higher had any integrity at all, this was an opportunity to bring the fears in my mind to the attention of my heart. I observed nature and the vivid panorama of red rock and sky. My mind ultimately yielded to a spacious stillness directed to my heart.

Before I knew it, I was back at my car. Safe. Unharmed. I knew in that moment that if I had fallen off the edge of the cliff and no one found me, nature would have taken care. My body could have dissolved into the Earth's embrace or been an animal's sustenance. I knew with certainty that although my body will die someday, an eternal being cannot be hurt. My purpose, revealed in that time and place, is that I am to live from my heart with the knowledge that I am an eternal being.

Returning to the Kogi with a Sister Traveler

Enlightened and empowered from my time in Sedona, I marveled at where my spiritual journey would take me next. Incidentally, it took me back to the Kogi with a woman who would end up playing a central role in my journey to liberation. You see, we were in a similar stage of life, Eva and me, searching for our purpose and what's really important. Beyond the basic bucket list of what we'd like to do while living on this earth, we were interested in exploring the long-held belief that human beings have the capacity to gain awareness of that part of themselves that is eternal, the soul. That everlasting spirit that never dies. Together, we began a mutual quest for ancient knowledge about the universe and our place in it.

Eva and I really clicked when I got back from my Sedona trip and told her about my wish to meet the Kogi again in South America. Her automatic response was, "I'm going too." Nine months later, World Healing Inc. offered a small group excursion to Colombia to be among the Kogi. This would be a once in a lifetime opportunity for westerners to go to the heart of the world on a shamanic journey. We would walk with elders up a great mountain, visit sacred sites, participate in thousand-year-old ceremonies, and listen to ancient teachings. Eva and I were dizzied with excitement! We were going on this trip.

After months of planning, we boarded our flight to Bogota, Colombia before sunup on a peaceful morning in March (2013). We spent the night in the city and rode a bus the next day to the Matuy Nature Reserve, part of the ancestral Kogi land that runs from the Atlantic Ocean to the lower Sierra Nevada de Santa Marta. There were twelve of us on this sacred expedition, a cadre of three men and nine women from around the world. Dazed, confused and exhausted after several days of travel, we finally arrived. Paradise would be our home for the next week. We'd linger on a sprawling, sandy beach by day and sleep in a thatched roof, bamboo hut at night. We were all there to learn from the wise, indigenous people who saw the world through a lens different from our own.

Eva and I anticipated the educational process from a western perspective: listen, reflect, ask questions, clarify. We got much more than an exacting curriculum and answers to our questions. The Mamos and other tribesmen communicated through a double translation process (Kogi to Spanish, to English). Whenever one of us westerners asked a question or made a comment, a group of eight elders pondered and explored the idea in depth, weighing each viewpoint until they settled on a response. When we were not formally engaged, the tribesmen remained in their open thatched tent about ten yards away. We could mutually observe one another. As we bathed ourselves in the presence of the Kogi and their culture, we discovered principles for living that have universal import.

For instance, we learned that these gentle people trust that love, respect, and gratitude lead the way in all experiences. Reaching consensus in formal discussions showed us how the tribe prioritizes the whole over the part, the group more than the individual. Whenever they ate, each member held and offered their food first to the heavens and then to their hearts before putting it in their mouths. This is a sign of gratitude and a prayer for blessings. Dressed in white to represent the purity of nature, the Great Mother, their unity symbolizes a commitment to preserve our ecosystems.

On our second day, we took a walk with the elders into the rainforest. Here, we received a teaching on the sacredness of the natural world. Everything is alive and spiritual, even that which is inanimate. The Kogi acknowledged every plant, animal, body of water, and landform they encountered. Such mindful attention to seemingly insignificant things exposed a central Kogi belief: the purpose of time is to provide the space for love and regard for nature and all beings. In slowing down to honor the life world around them, they join with something eternal.

Kogi Mamos; Colombia, South America

As I tried to follow the lead of my hosts and walk more attentively, I developed a deep appreciation for my place in the universe. I exist on a continuum of life with the air I breathe and the grounds upon which I tread. When the group stopped at a pool of holy water to look upon ancient rock formations with petroglyphs made by Kogi ancestors, I recognized the significance of honoring the past. Similar inscriptions have been discovered in other parts of the world to tell the histories of indigenous peoples.

Petroglyphs: History of the Kogi Mamos

The pinnacle of the trip was on day four when the eldest of the Mamos, who is in his nineties, led us on a steady, fast-paced climb to sacred ruins. The National Forest confiscated this holy land many years earlier, and the tribe hoped to regain legal control to protect the site. During the eleven-hour hike, our merry band of explorers climbed over boulders taller than we were and slogged ankle deep through thick mud and slop. Eva's shoes kept sucking off as she lifted her foot out of the mud. She ended up walking barefoot. We helped each other up and down the terrain until we reached level ground near the ocean where we swam and relaxed.

The Kogi taught us through their Being-ness, not their words. Rapt in the enormous spirits of these tiny beings in their homeland, we witnessed a reverence for all of life. Seeing the Mamos's love and respect for nature and each other was a chance for seekers like us to reunite with ageless wisdom and remember our true essence. Our connection with these people helped me to understand the concept that we are all one, *all part of the totality of life*. This inspired even as it demonstrated what is possible for the world. Spending time with the Kogi left my head and heart overflowing with experiences too numerous and complex to understand or explain. Eva and I went home with a truly sacred blessing, a milestone in our spiritual journey together.

**Eva Hunter; Karen Ibarguen Meditating at
the Ocean; Colombia, South America**

The Direct Experience of Being

> All the mind-streams eventually flow into the
> One ocean Beingness. There are many pathways
> for the mind; there are no paths for the Heart,
> for the Heart is infinite and fills everything.

Mooji, Author of Vaster Than Sky, Greater Than Space

After we returned from Colombia, Eva and I were more excited than ever to keep searching for the truth of who we really are. More than acknowledging that we exist as human beings living mundane lives, we were absorbed in the meaning of life itself. We contemplated that eternal question, "Who am I?" with the desire to gain recognition and direct experience of Beingness, or presence of Being. Sages have been asking themselves this question for thousands of years through contemplative self-inquiry. We were now part of that lineage.

One of Eva's out-of-town friends was part of a small group of seekers also practicing self-inquiry. They regularly discussed philosophical and spiritual videos, and shared information and personal testimony to inform their meditation. She was the one to introduce us to the video teachings of a spiritual holy man named Mooji.[10] His message of bringing meditative focus to the heart to discover higher consciousness resonated with both of us. We watched his videos over and over again.

Mooji's given name is Anthony Paul Moo-Young. Transplanted from Jamaica to England, he was drawn to religious practice after having a profound spiritual awakening with a Christian mystic. Shortly thereafter, he left his job and his home to start a life of simplicity. At times penniless, he spent the next six years absorbed in meditation. His joy and contentment led him to India where he serendipitously met three devotees of the enlightened master and his soon-to-be-guru Sri H.W.L. Poonja – known to his many followers as Papaji. Papaji was a disciple of the renowned Indian sage Bhagavan Sri Ramana Maharshi and believed intellectual understandings of spiritual liberation to be insufficient. True liberation, he expounded, came from experiencing one's essence directly.

The teachings of Mooji and his gurus draw upon the advaita tradition (also known as advaita vedanta), which is part of an ancient Hindu philosophy. The idea in advaita that human beings can access their eternal natures through direct experience stems from the principle of *non-duality* which means "not two" or "no separation." Nonduality is the sense that all things are interconnected while at the same time retaining their individuality. True Being exists beyond the mental constructs of personal identity and ego. From the advaita perspective, the direct experience of 'being' is what it truly means to be liberated.

Whenever something increases a person's direct experience of being, it opens the heart and quiets the mind. When I ponder the question: "Who is the 'I' that exists?" I, too, can sense my existence. I sometimes get a glimpse of my Beingness in meditation when my mind is quiet. Yet when I ask myself the question 'Who am I? my frustrated mind gets in the way of my sense of presence. Stuck in its ego-centric self, the mental construct of "I" keeps me working to answer the question with language and logic, when the eternal Self exists beyond both. On those occasions when I sit in stillness and happen upon my Beingness I realize, if only haphazardly, that there must be a way for me to deepen this experience, or make it more consistent.

Finding the truth of ourselves had become a pressing matter for Eva and me. We wanted to keep it front and center even though jobs, families and schedules don't leave much room for contemplating the eternal formlessness of one's existence. No wonder many sages seek years of solitude. In lieu of that, we watched hundreds of Mooji's teachings on video and spent hours in meditative self-inquiry. One day when we were discussing one of his teachings, we recognized that being in Mooji's presence would guide our inner work more effectively.

On Retreat in Portugal

In September (2013) Eva and I went to Portugal for a 7-day silent retreat to be with Mooji. There we were again, my soul sister and me, traveling the world in search of spiritual awakening. In truth, we were already *awake*. We just wanted to learn more about how to stay that way while living in our human bodies and a modern world. We have much to learn from ancient teachings and so little time that sometimes going far away to go inward is vital.

Eva and I boarded our flight and had a two-hour layover in New Jersey before heading off to Portugal. We were ecstatic about finally getting to meet Mooji in person. After 11 ½ hours and nearly 5000 miles in the air, we arrived in Lisbon at 8:30 AM. We and twenty other souls loaded a bus and rode to our retreat center in a southwestern part of the country. After we checked in, we unpacked our gear into the tents that would be our home for the next six nights. There was just enough time for lunch and a short rest before going to the orientation.

The massive tent had one main gathering area could hold more than 400 people. We mingled with the crowd in anticipation of what was to come. It was exciting to see people from all over the world with different religious and cultural backgrounds together in one place to learn from a great spiritual teacher.

After a brief introduction about the logistics for the week, Mooji entered. Everyone stood in awe of this small, sturdy man who lit up the room with his presence. He really did have a glow about him. He walked deliberately, touching the hands of audience members as he moved toward the stage. In his welcome, he said something about how "we are here to look beyond who we think we are." Eva and I were enchanted. We couldn't remember anything else he said.

A bell rang to signal everyone (participants and staff included) to begin a week of silence. The only time we were allowed to talk was during Satsang (when participants as a group engage in spiritual dialogue with a guru). During this six-day period of reflection, contemplation, and self-inquiry, we were not to gesture or communicate in any way. Lack of contact encouraged each of us to focus on our internal space and notice challenges that the mind and body present.

We didn't even talk during meals. We ate mindfully, chewing each bite of food to explore its taste, smell, and texture while appreciating its sustenance and what went into its preparation. From the fertile seeds to the tending, harvesting and threshing of mature grains, to the hauling, drying, stacking, bagging, soaking, cooking, and serving. That was just the rice! I looked forward to each scrumptious meal. Eating in silent contemplation, I was aware of the chain of life and the collaboration involved in the most fundamental aspects of daily activity.

Still, it was unusual not to say hello, have eye contact, or acknowledge people around me. I had a yearning to go outside of myself especially with Eva, my partner on this spiritual journey. If we passed each other in the dining room, as we did on occasion, we'd put our hands to our hearts and tip our heads down in acknowledgement. I loved those slight interactions even though we weren't supposed to have them. I never would have imagined being with a group of people for a week without communicating like this. The experience was profound. I seek out moments of silence each day to remember the essence and continuity of life.

Mooji led two Satsangs each day where we all gathered for several hours to hear his teachings, ask questions, meditate, and sing bhajan, (Sanskrit for devotional singing). The word is derived from the root *bhaj*, which means "to divide, share, partake, participate, to belong to." Based in Hindu tradition, bhajans are usually lyrical and refer to key themes in ancient teachings.

We often opened or closed our gatherings with the mantra, *Om*. This mystic syllable appears at the beginning and end of most Sanskrit recitations, prayers, and texts and is considered to be the most sacred mantra in Hinduism and Tibetan Buddhism as well as other religions. Composed of the three sounds a-u-m, *Om* mystically embodies the essence of the entire universe. This meaning is further deepened by the Hindu belief that God first created a vibration, out of which sound and the universe arose. As the most sacred sound, the vibration Om is the root of the universe, the frequency that joins all things.

The Bhajans we sang together were so uplifting and fulfilling that my heart sang even though my head at the time didn't know what they meant. One of my favorites was and is *Sita Ram / Jai Jai Ram*. Sita refers to the incarnation of Spirit/Lord as light, strength, and virtue, representing the feminine. Ram denotes the embodiment of the Spirit/Lord as light, strength, and virtue, epitomizing the masculine. Jai means victory. Together, the mantra asks for blessings: 'May the Lord as light, strength, and virtue that dwells in my heart be victorious over all obstacles (internal and external).' Every time we sang and danced together, I felt kinship with everyone there, and to something higher.

Another one of my favorites is *Om Namo Bhagavate Vasudevya*. This mantra means 'Salutations to Lord Vishnu.' Based in the Sanskrit root 'vish,' Lord Vishnu means 'that which pervades the Universe.' In other words, it refers to the universal. *That cosmic ocean which permeates all things.* A Vedic astrologer who read my birth chart several years ago told me this sacred mantra would assist me in my journey toward liberation in this life. I felt a powerful connection to it even then, though I didn't grasp its meaning at first.

Eva and I sometimes sat next to each other during the Satsangs. Mostly we were within eye shot of one another. I liked knowing she was there and sensing her presence as we traveled our individual yet mutual paths of self-inquiry. During one of the Satsangs, I listened intently as she and Mooji had a brief exchange about meditation and observing the mind.

> Eva: "It's easy for me to sit as the observer and watch my mind, even though my mind will pull me out and create all these dances for me to do, like washing the dishes, calling somebody on the phone, and so on. My question is: Although I am aware of, and comfortable with this observer, there is something expansive *behind* it, something I sense. It does not have a shape or sound, or

anything of the five senses. Yet I do sense it. I am aware of it. **What is *that?*"**

Mooji: "Don't worry about that. Just be with it."

When I asked Eva after the retreat what she thought about Mooji's response, she told me she remembered thinking to herself, "That's not any help!" We still laugh about it.

Even though I never spoke up during the Satsangs, I always felt like Mooji was speaking to me directly. It was as though every comment or question someone asked was a query straight from my subconscious mind. Mooji's responses always gave me clarity.

At the end of the last Satsang, we took turns meeting with him in the front of the room to get a blessing and some camphor. We'd use the camphor in a burning ceremony as a symbol of burning away all that we are not. That day he sneaked a small statue of Buddha into Eva's hand and whispered into her ear, "This will be easy for you." Tears of love and joy streamed down her face. I felt such delight seeing Mooji acknowledge her in such a way. My dear, Eva!

Mooji led several guided meditations during the retreat as well. At the end of one of them, I was overcome with such emotion that I sobbed. I wasn't the only one. I could hear others with stuttering breath and sniffling noses. I looked up to see Eva standing to leave the pavilion with the crowd. I couldn't follow. The enormous opening in my heart did not dissipate. I fell back to my mat and cried until I couldn't cry anymore, my tears encircled within a mass of 400 loving people. I felt such peace and stillness after that. After I finally rolled myself up to a seated position, I spent another 15 minutes sitting. After I got my bearings, I stood up and floated to my tent with a lightness of body and calmness of mind. I fell into a deep sleep within seconds of putting my head to the pillow.

On another occasion, the emotional response that surfaced was not sadness. It was furious anger. I don't know what provoked it or if it just arose on its own. We were in the midst of Satsang. It was not the time or place to deal with it. I allowed myself to feel the anger and told myself, as if speaking to it directly, "I will mentally bookmark you and get back to this sensation and emotion when I get back to my tent." I knew the anger was part of me, and I wanted to respect it for holding space in my body for my protection. That is what stored memories and emotions do: they protect. Anything can trigger them.

As soon as Satsang ended, I walked back to my tent by myself. When I arrived, I tried to think through my feelings. It didn't work. All I could do was scream into my pillow, my shrieks muffled so as not to disturb anyone. Anger gave way to tears. The armor I'd worn since my childhood was beginning to crack. The terror and grief underneath needed to escape. As the horror revealed itself and then started to dissolve, I allowed myself to feel it in all of its forms. I breathed into it. After about twenty minutes, peace and spaciousness drifted into my heart.

I was under no illusion that my childhood wounds were all healed. Yet the embodied emotional release of what had been festering for decades gave me a new sense of myself. I knew that it was the silence of the retreat coupled with meditation and energized Satsang that allowed me to look at myself completely. I could finally ask, "Who is the "I" that exists in this body and lives this life?" Mooji's teachings made more sense than ever. "The operation of consciousness has created the *apparition* called *me*"[11] As I peeled away more of that illusive, egoistic identity that masquerades as myself, I touched the eternal.

When Eva and I boarded the plane for our 25-hour trip back to Texas via a Frankfurt layover, we had very different conceptions of who we were than when we first arrived. In fact, I wasn't really ready to go home. I was fundamentally changed. I didn't know how I would reintegrate with my life there. I did, and so did Eva. While the experience stayed with us as we continued our self-inquiry, we yearned to spend more time in our guru's presence. When Mooji posted an opening a few months later for volunteers to join him and his team in southern Portugal that next summer (2014), we both applied. Eva offered her body-work, kitchen or cleaning help, and I offered the construction help. I was still waiting for my reply a few weeks later when Eva received an email from the team that said they only needed construction help at that time. They were thankful for her application and told her that she could reapply at a future date. I was disappointed. I knew that this may put us on different paths. At the same time, I also knew that we would continue our self-inquiry and healing work whether or not I was accepted into the Karma Yoga program.

When I Became Sanoja

Mooji's home at Monte Sahaja, Portugal is a living Ashram where people gather for periods of time for spiritual inquiry – to search for the truth of who they are. One of Mooji's offerings at the ashram is a two-week Karma Yoga program. Karma yoga, based on the teachings of a sacred Sanskrit scripture of Hinduism called the *Bhagavad Gita*, is a discipline of selfless action or, a path to realization by doing for others without expectation of benefits (such as fame or other personal merits). As a form of yoga, selfless action purifies the mind, creates inner peace, and forges a sense of oneness with God and all humanity.

The Monte Sahaja team put out a request for people with expertise in construction to volunteer their time to expand the Ashram. I had the experience they needed. I owned and operated a roofing business for 15 years before becoming a chiropractor and Reiki healer. I heartily submitted my application. Three months later I had a Skype interview and was accepted into the program. They wanted me to go to the site for one month during the summer of 2014 to organize and maintain a central hub for the construction teams. I would have an opportunity to practice Karma Yoga with Mooji himself.

In addition to managing the construction hub, maintaining inventory, and keeping the weekly supplies on order, I built a storage shed and other small items as needed. Knowing that I had a background in chiropractic and Reiki, several of the workers asked me for treatments. I loved having a chance to use my therapeutic skills while I was there. I'd work until lunch with the construction team, eat in silence, then go to temple for a one-hour meditation and prayers. Having a meal in silence rather than chattering away was a means to stay focused on my internal work. Then I'd treat patients until dinner. It was a long day. I treasured how mutually supportive it was to combine selfless service and spiritual introspection.

At the end of the first week, one of Mooji's assistants rang the bell at breakfast to announce a *naming ceremony* to be held the following night. We were all invited. A naming ceremony is when a guru (meaning 'weighty one' in Sanskrit) gives a devotee a new name. It is meant to assist their journey of self-inquiry and typically occurs after a period of intensive time together. The name represents a symbolic rebirth and may take the form of an attribute, name, or identity of the Divine. Mooji received his new name many years ago.

"The pronounced sound 'mu' in Japanese, comes from the root Chinese word 'wu' meaning emptiness, nothingness. 'Ji': this Hindi term is used at the end of a name as a mark of respect and affection. Sri Mooji prefers this name and sound, which is already part of his family name, to the personal Christian name 'Tony.'" [11]

After some consideration, I asked one of Mooji's assistants if I could get a new name. It was a long shot. Mooji was known for working with people sometimes longer than a year before sanctifying them in this way. I'd spent time with him on retreat and felt ready to infuse my spiritual quest with blessings from this soul who had become my guru (teacher). I didn't know if he'd think I was ready. I was elated to find out the next morning that I'd be one of nine people to be given a new name.

The night of the naming ceremony, Mooji opened with prayers and explained why someone might want to have a spiritual name and why it may be beneficial. The new name works in concert with the bearer's spiritual goals and helps to engender further awakening. On the path to spiritual enlightenment, identifying with a new name marks a significant change and point of no return. When imbued with spiritual energy, the name itself is thought to confer the character it represents. It's also a great motivator for staying on one's path.

Those of us receiving spiritual names waited in anticipation to be called, one by one, to the front of the room. Eight of my peers went before me, each kneeling before our Guruji, (a personal spiritual teacher) to receive prayers and a new name. After accepting the name, they returned to their seats. I was the last one to be called. Like the others, I rested my knees on a cushion in front of Mooji with my hands together at my heart. He said some words to the group then a prayer and told me my name is Sanoja (Sanskrit for eternal), followed by a lighthearted "Get used to it!" After I agreed to the name, there was a long pause. Our eyes locked as Mooji said, "You are the one I've been waiting for." I was startled, almost shocked as my expression didn't change. My mind was still and I felt we were looking into each other's soul. I slowly smiled, bowing in gratitude and devotion as he cradled my head in his hands.

After concluding my part of the service, Mooji spoke briefly to the group and offered prayers. Then I joined the others. We ended the ceremony singing the mantra *Om Namah Shivaya* as a form of prayer. In East Indian mythology, Shiva is the name given to the Consciousness that dwells in everything, human beings included. *Om Namah Shivaya* means, "I bow to Shiva, my inner Self: Consciousness." I beamed with renewed reverence to my own soul. When we finished, all nine of us received hugs and congratulations from all who witnessed our naming.

My new name was significant. Sanoja, the eternal. The weight of Mooji's *other* words tugged at me. I wanted to know what he meant when he said I was the one he'd been waiting for.

The next day I asked Mooji's personal assistant if I could have a meeting with him. "He doesn't take personal meetings. All questions need to be raised during Satsang." I accepted the response, but my question was personal. I thought it might be inappropriate for the group setting. So, I never asked and never found out what Mooji meant. In hindsight, it didn't matter. I wasn't there to discover my personal self, Karen. I was there to discover *Sanoja*, the one who signifies my eternal nature, which goes beyond ego and identity. I imagine Mooji knew his words would bring me to this realization.

After being immersed in the community at Monte Sahaja for five weeks, I returned home full of joy and peace of mind. Maintaining this state of Beingness amid the normal workings of everyday life would be a challenge. The mind is a powerful source for moving away from one's true nature. To integrate my discoveries into daily living, I set aside more time each day to meditate and contemplate. I revised my work schedule so that I could center myself throughout the day—to align with my breath, declutter my mind, and give attention to the present moment.

Letting go of the illusion of control allowed life to unfold without my having to plan every detail. This approach, though freeing in many ways, had to be incorporated slowly. Control was ingrained into who I thought I was, the controller of life. Sanoja needed to remind me continuously that I am yet eternal.

Return to Monte Sahaja, Portugal

Early the next spring, I received an invitation from Mooji and the *sangha* (community, in Sanskrit) to return to Portugal to help with another construction project. They wanted to get the Monte Sahaja property prepared for two consecutive 10-day silent retreats for 400 people each. They offered me a three-month visit. I got my tickets and passport, packed my tent and equipment, and arranged for my usual substitute doctor to treat my patients while I would be away. All of the paperwork was in order. The ten-weeks construction project at the Ashram were nothing like the Karma Yoga program I participated in a year earlier. We worked 6½ days per week with a half-day of Satsang on Sundays. I was up at 6:00 AM, got dressed and finished breakfast by 7:00 AM, and met with the construction crew for our morning meeting. We oriented new volunteers and split into project teams. I managed supplies and inventory, built storage racks, organized materials, and made sure each team had the equipment they needed.

It was a physical and stressful job that pushed me to the edges of my capacity physically, mentally and emotionally. We worked long hours in hot temperatures under tight deadlines. While the food was delicious, it didn't have enough calories to sustain the high level of exertion. I took to eating chocolate every day for immediate boosts of energy. I still lost weight over the ten weeks. As I weakened, I realized that part of what sustained me during the previous year's outing was my healing work. I'd done chiropractic and Reiki treatments that helped me to maintain equilibrium. Without it, I was in a state of imbalance.

I wasn't the only person suffering from frustration and exhaustion. Tensions occasionally flared. For one, I had a spat with one of Mooji's staff members over a miscommunication about supplies. It was my job to find out what the construction crews needed each week and put in an order. It was his job make the purchase. When some of the materials and equipment never arrived, I inquired. Turns out that he skipped part of the order. "Order it next week!" he said.

I was furious. If the crews don't have what they need to expand the main facility, build showers and bathrooms, erect tent platforms, construct retaining walls and steps, among other things, the whole construction plan falls behind. What's more, following up on random missing items from each purchase order falls outside my job description. After raising my voice and going back and forth with him for a few minutes, I just asked him to be proactive and find extra help if that's what he needed. He said okay. We were all weary and knew we needed to be compassionate with each other. We hugged and had good communication after that.

We finished the construction just in time for first the 10-day retreat. Literally. The participants arrived in waves the next morning. It was a relief to be done with it. I was exhausted from ten weeks of nonstop labor and the teams pulling me in multiple directions. I didn't have a chance to debrief with myself or anyone else about the experience. I just let out a deep sigh.

When the participants arrived, I was on the welcoming team. I greeted them and gave them the lay of the land as I took them to their tent or cabin. It was hot in Portugal that summer with several days over 100 degrees. We melted as we walked.

The next morning was my first day in the kitchen. I was up at 5:00 AM, and breakfast started at 6:00 AM. It was hectic because we could not break the quiet of this silent retreat even though we were the staff who needed to communicate for logistical reasons. The crew and I fumbled around to find where food was stored after the evening crew restocked it. We wrote questions and answers on scraps of paper in a soundless dialogue. We washed fruit, cooked porridge and eggs, toasted bread, sliced cheese, pulled out the homemade jelly, and prepared Muesli with almond or soy milk. Somehow breakfast got served to the staff and 400 visitors from around the globe. It all became routine after a while.

I finished in the kitchen just before 10:00 AM each day and hurried over to the Mooji Mandir (Temple) for morning Satsang, 'Gatherings for Truth' with the Guru. When I laid eyes on the newly erected temple for the first time, I reveled. It was stunning. I felt humbled to have worked with the skilled and industrious construction teams who built it. I recalled the months of sweat and labor involved as Mooji appeared in the distance. Riding along in his golf cart, he and his driver approached the facility. I went in to join the others.

We stood in reverence as Mooji entered the Mandir (temple). He had such a presence. It was as though we could breathe him in. Satsang began right away. People asked their questions; Mooji offered his answers; the rest of us contemplated the questions as if they were our own. Often, they were. The session went on for more than two hours. Mooji stood up, bowed, and put his hands to his forehead in a prayer position as he tenderly scanned the crowd with soft, brown eyes. He greeted the crowds as he strolled out of the temple, his love palpable. Off he went in his buggy to the other side of the property where he lived.

I'd usually stay in the Mandir after Satsang to meditate, along with the other lingerers who liked to take advantage of the energy encircling its majestic walls. After about 15 minutes, I'd walk mindfully to the dining area in anticipation of the meal to come. The chef prepared organic dishes, freshly made bread, salad, and vegetables. We'd have several choices for the entrée, including pasta, curry and other ethnic foods. Following the general tradition of eating like a king for breakfast, a prince for lunch, and a pauper for dinner, the evening meal was light and simple. Salad, cheese, bread, and vegetables.

We'd have a three- to four-hour break between the morning and afternoon Satsangs. After lunch, there were several designated areas for contemplation and meditation within walking distance. Most days, I'd go back to the temple for about an hour before wandering the property. I'd find a bench or swing, nap under a shade tree, gaze out at the lake, or try to spot fish in the pond. I'd usually end up at my tent to rest in privacy. It was under a

shade tree and offered reprieve from the sweltering sun. Then it was time for the afternoon Satsang.

I was wiped out by the end of each day. I'd take a quick bucket shower with heated water to get the dust and sweat off, then go to bed. Unfortunately, the three-person tent that I lugged all the way from Texas and used during the construction part of my trip was replaced with a two-person tent provided by the retreat. I couldn't sit up. I had to crouch to move around. When I asked about using my own tent, the staff declined saying that they wanted them to be uniform. I didn't understand. The tent I brought with me blended into the terrain better than theirs did.

It's funny how life works. I had food, shelter, community, and a chance for guided self-inquiry. What else did I need? An opportunity to practice tolerance and allowance of whatever occurs apparently. I noticed my desire to control and rationalize the tent situation. Acceptance was a simple matter of changing perspective. Lesson learned, though I'd surely learn it again many times over.

The star-filled skies and crisp night-time breezes lulled me into deep relaxation at the end of full days. Regardless, I couldn't seem to catch up on the rest I lost from the first leg of the trip. I was tired when I awoke each day at 5:00 AM. That fatigue accumulated throughout each day and spilled into the next. By the end of the retreat I was thoroughly exhausted.

When everything was over, I spent two days at the Ashram to rest. I went to the temple for meditation and prayer, meandered around the property, and reflected on everything that happened during my time there. I felt wrung out and full of gratitude to

have spent ten weeks with Mooji and the Sangha. I was ready to go home.

On the morning of my departure, I hurried from the dining room to see Mooji sitting in the driver's seat of his golf cart. He was waiting in the main area reserved for arrivals and departures when he called me over. We hugged, and I whispered heartfelt thanks for his presence and 'pointings' as he calls them. He held my hand and uttered a few words to me and the group about the Heart Sutra; I don't remember the specific words. I felt such unconditional love and compassion emanating from him that tears welled in my eyes. I lowered my head, my body pulsing in sync with the slow rhythm of my cries. The word "aww" floated from the crowd.

Mooji spoke his wisdom for another twenty minutes. I stood as close as I could as he held my arm with a loving caress. His assistant stepped out of the passenger's seat to let us share this rare time together. After we hugged our final goodbyes, I drew my hands together at my heart in a gesture of reverence and bowed in gratitude and love. Mooji smiled and drove off in his little cart. I hugged everyone before hopping into the van to catch my train to Lisbon for the trip back home.

The wide-open heart, tranquil mind, and subtle awareness that revealed itself by the end of my time at the Ashram stayed with me. It was the first time I'd felt my *true nature* as an Eternal Being for a sustained period of time. I started back to my day job ten days after landing in Texas. Living from my heart space, my life had changed.

Chapter 3

CLEARING OUT THE IMPRINTS OF TRAUMA

On an autumn night in the mid-80's, I drove to Oklahoma to take part in a North American Indian pow-wow. This annual festival of feasting, dancing and singing is both secular and sacred, a time of fellowship, joy, and spirituality for tribal members and guests. The friend who invited me was, like her mother, of Native American ancestry. I don't recall which of the thirty-nine federally recognized tribes in Oklahoma they were part of. I do remember that it was important to them that they honor and preserve their tribal culture, and share it with me.

As soon as I arrived at the celebration my friend's mother solemnly wrapped a hand-made shawl around my shoulders. It is customary to give a gift to each person participating in the ceremony as a sign of respect and honor. I received her gesture warmly and stared into the fire pit at the center of the dance circle. Flames stretched like long, pointy fingers into the twilight.

The lead dancers were swathed in feathered headdresses,

with jingling bells around their ankles. They danced a complete circle before I inched over to join in. My stockinged feet sank into sandy soil as I shuffled in time to the beat. I lowered my head to listen carefully and absorb the vibrations of sacred chants and heavy drums. Reverberations ricocheted through my muscles, organs and bones until my heart seemed to tune to the whole of life itself. The animated crowd whirled with a light-heartedness that only comes from being fully present. Words were unnecessary. Our *beingness* was beyond the limits of language or thought. That experience was one of the earliest glimpses I'd had into multiple planes of existence. I've been intrigued with ancient traditions ever since.

A Modern-Day Shaman

More than three decades after my introduction to Native culture and its transformative potential I met Kevin Snow, the Desert Shaman.[12] A Shaman is an intermediary who uses tools for intuitive guidance to intercede with the cosmic order on someone's behalf. Shamans have been central to native spirituality, intuitive guidance, and healing for thousands of years. Traditionally, they were priests and doctors known colloquially as medicine men and medicine women. Their role was to secure the help of the spirit world for the benefit of individuals and communities. Though there are fewer shamans in the modern era even among tribal peoples, the tradition has been passed down for centuries and has gained entry into select present-day healing modalities. Kevin is one such contemporary.

Kevin Snow has studied the Shamanic tradition extensively with Native American teachers and has been involved in the healing arts for more than twenty years. He holds a Bachelor's degree in psychology, is pursuing a Master's degree in counseling, and has certificates in Reiki and yoga. I met him at a workshop in October, 2015 and had several private sessions with him to aid in my personal journey. I witnessed first-hand how he uses ancient and modern practices to guide self-healing. As a modern-day shaman, communicating with other realms of existence guides his therapeutic approach even as his expertise in transpersonal psychology informs it.

You see, shamans communicate with three distinct *worlds* (realms) –middle, upper, and lower. The 'middle world' refers to the material or practical realm in which we live. This includes the challenges and experiences of everyday life. The 'Upper World' involves loving beings who once held human form and now exist as *angels and spirit guides* who assist the middle world. Shamans might access the energy of Buddha, Christ, the Divine Mother, the Great Spirit (an expression of universal spiritual force), saints and others for guidance or to promote energetic balance. The 'lower world' encompasses *elementals*, or *nature guides*, such as plants (e.g., the sacred tobacco medicine or essential oils) and animals (e.g., the eagle, buffalo, bear, or wolf) that connote behaviors or qualities in accord with a tribal culture's beliefs. For example, the eagle represents vision and the buffalo, abundance.

Grounded in presence and clear intention, the shaman knows *who* to talk to and *what* to ask. The information acquired from these realms may come in the form of visions, sounds and smells, or thoughts, feelings, sensations and other ways of knowing. The shaman is responsible for understanding and implementing the messages received.

Shamans might also use Tarot and Oracle cards to gain insight to create a plan for healing and spiritual growth. Dating back to the middle ages and created by artists and spiritual teachers, Tarot and oracle decks come in a variety of themes from Victorian Era floral designs to the Lord of the Rings. Visionary artist Robert Place illustrated his Alchemical Tarot deck in the style of original Renaissance alchemical art.[13] Kevin uses multiple decks in his healing work including: Alchemical Tarot, Archangel Raphael Healing Oracle Cards, Ascended Masters Oracle, Animal Totems, Spirit of the Wheel, Medicine Wheel, Stones, a Goddess deck and an Archetype deck.

Regardless of motif, every 78-card Tarot deck has a numerical ordering that corresponds with *developmental cycles in life*. Divided into two parts, major and minor 'arcana' (or, profound secrets), the cards help to explain the universe and our place in it. The 56 cards in the minor arcana represent the *activities and concerns of our everyday lives* whereas the major arcana (with 22 cards) symbolize the archetypes of human experience. These are the cards that form the foundation of the deck and contain *major life lessons*. The Fool, for example, is either unnumbered or marked zero. Representing the innocence of beginnings, The Fool is like a newborn, inexperienced yet eager to venture out into the world in blissful innocence. The World card (# 21) on the other hand denotes a more complete understanding of the world, an integration of disparate parts as a person, *once a fool, becomes whole and fulfilled with his or her life's purpose.*[14]

Artist: Robert M. Place
The Alchemical Tarot Deck by Robert M. Place

Oracle cards emerged around the 19th century in Europe and, like Tarot decks, are available in variety of themes. Quite different from Tarot, however, oracle cards do not rely on a numerical progression. They are based instead in the numerological principle that numbers, and all things for that matter, vibrate in a precise mathematical way.[15] They also attract similar vibrational frequencies. In this way, *thoughts and feelings (as vibrational energies) become manifest.* The cards help to reveal what energies are at work in a person's life, as each one has significance as the reader interprets a word or image on the card drawn.

Communicating with other realms through cards or channeling is really a form of energy transfer. Thought or prayer is a form of subtle energy, not wholly unlike that of the nervous system or a molecule of water with its protons and electrons. Thus, healers might access the three worlds through energy channels to promote physical and emotional self-healing through energy transference. Reiki practitioners sense and shift the flow of energy in themselves and their clients. Similarly, shamans might draw upon energetic forces to balance chakras (those subtle energy centers of the body), remove energetic blockages, clear out negative energy, and rebalance the spiritual, mental, emotional or physical aspects of a person. The information sent and received (as energy) encourages healthy energy flow by clearing out imbalances and negative energy.

For example, to center himself prior to a healing session, Kevin focuses his awareness on Christ energy and mindfully moves through each of his chakras to sense alignment or misalignment. If the energy is out of whack, he asks Christ energy to restore balance. When he feels that the chakras are clear, he similarly assesses the physical, mental, emotional, and spiritual aspects of his body to clear out perceived imbalances. Finally, he brings his attention to the setting he is in. If he experiences negative energy there, he asks Christ energy to clear it out. Kevin uses this protocol periodically during a session with a client to make sure that he and the environment are balanced and free of negative energy.

In addition to sensing energy, Kevin uses a pendulum. This instrument relies on gravity and momentum in response to energy. Its swing changes direction in relation to energetic forces. When the shaman asks a specific question, they monitor the movement of the pendulum to discern the answer. In the case of a simple yes or no question, the pendulum swings in one direction to confirm the statement and in the opposite direction to refute it. This is one of many ways to use a pendulum to communicate with energetic realms. If the shaman is unsure of a result, they ask the question again to confirm.

The point of communicating with the three worlds is to use the information to help people to move their lives in an auspicious way. This includes but is not limited to healing the physical body. It's not as ethereal as it may sound. That a person's thoughts and focus have the power to create reality is an idea both ancient and modern. Consider this example:

> You're walking down the street. A lion appears out of nowhere and bounds toward you. Your body tightens; your heart beats faster; and your breath quickens to prepare for an impending attack. Fear kicks in, simultaneously transmitting incoming data to the amygdala (an almond shaped structure in the medial temporal lobe of the brain). *Danger! Attacker!* Once the information is received, the amygdala signals the creation of adrenalin so you can *fight* or *flee*. You choose one of those options in a split second. Regardless of the outcome, the entire lionesque experience is stored in that little, nut-shaped hard drive of

yours so that if something similar happens in the
future, you'll be prepared.

Here's where the personal power of creation comes in. Any
experience can be perceived as *equally life-threatening* to the attack
of the ferocious lion of doom whether or not this is actually
true. Walking down a similar-looking street, noticing sudden
movement in the distance, crossing paths with a lumbering St.
Bernard, and so on, if *perceived* as similar to the lion episode,
triggers that same reaction of fight or flight (along with the
thoughts, beliefs, emotions, and physical responses that
accompanied it).

This is how information gets stored in the body and can
continue to program the nervous system to respond in ways that
no longer fit the circumstances. The traumatic experience leaves
an impression in the physical, mental, emotional, and spiritual
aspects of a person. There's no need to be afraid of the gentle
canine giant. However, the trauma will continue to conjure up
fear and shape a person's reality unless it gets cleared out.

The Four Bodies

The illustration of the traumatic lion can be understood in
terms of a conceptual model called the *four bodies*. Instead of
being purely corporeal, the human body is comprised of spiritual,
mental, and emotional aspects. Although it may sound obvious
to some that thoughts, beliefs, emotions, and actions influence
how the human body physically functions, the physical body
would not exist without the other three. Even so, many of us

amble through our daily lives thinking that the physical body stands alone. It does not.

Figure 1: Four Body Quadrants and their Primary Content (below) offers a general explanation of how the spiritual, mental, emotional, and physical bodies influence one another and essentially create 'what is.'

Figure 1: Four Body Quadrants and their Primary Content

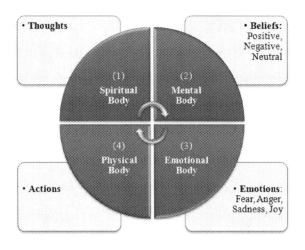

When the *spiritual body* (quadrant 1) endures painful experiences like even the 'thought' of being attacked by a lion, the *mental body* (quadrant 2) creates a 'belief' such as "The world is a dangerous place" or "I'm not good enough, fast enough, strong enough." *The emotional body* (quadrant 3) attaches the emotions of fear, anger, or sadness to those thoughts, beliefs, and overarching visions of the world and one's place in it. Then all of that content gets dumped into the *physical body* (quadrant 4) and manifests as health issues, hurtful relationships, suboptimal decisions, addictions, or inadvertently bringing about self-destructive results. In addition, *stress* is fundamentally a culmination of stored content in quadrants 1-3. When a stress response becomes the norm in a person's life, it continuously dumps that content into the physical body, keeping it in a constant state of imbalance. Not surprisingly, the content within the four bodies impacts relationships, decisions, behaviors, world view, self-concept, and virtually every other aspect of a human being. Physical manifestations such as shortness of breath, rapid heart rate, ulcers, headaches, minor illnesses, and diseases result.

The Four Bodies, Through the Eyes of the Desert Shaman

Kevin Snow believes that the primary content of each of the four bodies offers a gateway for finding energetic balance: *Thought* in the spiritual body; equals *belief* in the mental body; equals *emotion* in the emotional body; equals *action* in the physical body. By accessing the four bodies through intuitive processes, he assesses how emotions, thoughts, and beliefs impact the physical body and then recommends actions his clients can take to aid in their healing. The action is a way to communicate back to the spiritual realm that the client understands and is implementing the guidance received. The action itself catalyzes healing.

To make the four bodies framework more concrete, I'll share my experiences working with Kevin to revitalize and rebalance myself. He used shamanic healing techniques to help me to clear out the spiritual, mental, and emotional blocks manifesting in my physical body.

The Physical Body

According to the four bodies theory the spiritual, mental, and emotional bodies all dump their content into the physical body. Thus, the physical body can be a pathway to the other three. A healer or shaman can get a read on physicality by assessing a person's connection with the earth. Both the material and energetic composition of the body is comprised earth elements: Minerals, water, proteins, fats, carbohydrates. Connection to the earth is neither good nor bad. It is simply an indicator of polarity. When there is too little earth element, a person may feel disconnected from their own body, struggle with handling mundane tasks, or find it difficult to think concretely or get a grip on reality.

To find out how much *earth element* is generally present in a person, Kevin connects with the upper world using his pendulum. He channels the energy of the Divine Mother, symbolized by the earth, and asks how much earth element is present in that person. Using the pendulum, he offers a series of possible answers (e.g., 10, 20, 30 percent, and so on). When the direction of the pendulum swing changes, it indicates the answer. He keeps track of the numbers with his fingers and sometimes ends up counting to 100. In my session with him, the pendulum swing changed direction to indicate 90 percent. Put simply, this meant that I was not very grounded. I was not surprised.

Since the abuses of my early childhood, I'd become rather disembodied to protect myself from the feelings and emotions associated with the trauma. The distress from that experience existed outside of my mental body, beyond my conscious mind. The wound hid in the lower right quadrant of my abdomen, experienced physically as tightness and pain. The energy session I had with Eva that revealed 5-year-old Karen to me was the first time that scared, assaulted little girl tasted freedom. By acknowledging the pain and suffering I'd been carrying for all of those years, I started to reconnect with my physical body. Grounding myself would take more time.

Kevin had practical recommendations to assist my re-grounding. Rubbing Vetiver essential oil (also known as Khus) on my right foot for six days gave me an immediate feeling of calm with each use, along with a reason to prop my feet up and relax at the end of the day. He also suggested that I practice yoga and Tai Chi. By corresponding my movements with my breath, I started to reconnect myself to the present moment and balance my energies.

From both an energetic and biochemical standpoint, these actions make sense. Each of the body's major chakras is associated with specific locations in the body (such as the sacrum, the heart, the throat) and is governed by the underlying network of glands in the endocrine system. The endocrine system regulates hormones, making it the master of chemistry in the body and a controller of all body systems.

For instance, the sacral (2nd) chakra is related to the adrenal grands, which balance the hormones cortisol and adrenalin. In a state of fear or stress (in real times of danger or due to the imaginings left from the imprint of prior trauma), both of these hormones elevate to trigger and support the body's fight-or-flight response. When these hormone levels are too high over a period of time, they can increase blood sugar and cholesterol levels, decrease immunity, interfere with learning and memory, and contribute to a host of other negative health outcomes. Explained in terms of the four body quadrants: When thought in the *spiritual body* becomes a belief in the *mental body,* and that belief attaches to an emotion in the *emotional body,* it then becomes chemistry in the *physical body.* By noticing the physical body's sensations and holding them in the present moment, one can address the emotional, mental, and spiritual bodies.

To assist my meditations, Kevin asked me to shuffle the Alchemical Tarot card deck, place it on the table and draw a card to represent my physical body. I drew The *Hierophant* card (#5, major arcana), which represents healing, morality, interpreting life's mysteries and sacred truths, and the publishing of teachings. A Greek word for high priest, hierophant also represents action and great creativity. In a sense, this card would support my efforts to balance my physical body through inspired expression. And to focus my spiritual practice, he recommended that I connect with the energies of the archangel Raphael who is frequently identified with all matters involving physical health. According to *The Catholic Encyclopedia,* this speculation is based on the significance of the name, meaning "God has healed," and on the healing role attributed to Raphael in the Gospel of John and other spiritual texts, including those in Judaism and Islam.[16] Calling upon the archangel Raphael would help me to experience my body as healed, whole, and a blessing to the world.

The Emotional Body

The *emotional body* provides fertile ground for promoting balance and well-being or physical fragility and infirmity. An emotion can be thought about as a physiological manifestation of a feeling or as a sensation-based form of perception. This means that the emotional body contains one's current emotional state (fear, anger, sadness, joy) as well as sensations, perceptions, and the emotional imprints of significant memories and past experiences.

Regardless of the origins, an abundance of *anger, fear, and sadness* tends to diminish the joy in a person's life. When these negative emotions are minimal, joy is predominant. In truth, *joy* is the human being's primary state of being. Unlike the feeling of pleasure that comes from the sweet satisfaction of tasting your favorite ice cream, joy is a natural state of being that is predisposed to notice and attend to that which is wholesome and satisfying. In Joy, the simple act of breathing derives pleasure. This is not to say that emotions are good or bad, or that joy should negate or suppress the authentic expressions of anger, fear, or sadness. All genuine emotions, adequately processed in the body, serve the whole and allow one's awareness of presence to be revealed.

The buried trauma of my childhood unconsciously prepared me to look for danger and be ready to fight or flee. This emotional imprint put my physical body in a perpetual state of slight, constant contraction— as though my body were set to spring into action at any moment. My desire to go inward to uncover my spiritual self in some ways balanced this out and so did not diminish the joy in my life. In fact, Kevin sensed no anger or negative self-talk in my emotional body. There was instead an underlying presence of fear and sadness that I needed to clear out.

Dissipating emotional excess through the body is paramount for healing. Thousands of years ago when people walked everywhere, slept on the ground, tended to plants and animals, and constantly engaged with the natural world, they had ample opportunity to dissipate emotional content through their physical connection to the earth. This was not a utopian world without suffering or pain; it was a scenario in which human beings were grounded due to the circumstances of their lives. Today with more limited contact to the natural world, human beings are predisposed to function with excess emotional content, dumped into the physical body. Moving it through requires reconnecting to the earth and the earth elements within us.

Earthing techniques are a great way to do this. Feel the grass beneath your bare feet; take a walk in the park; feel the sunshine on your face. You might hold a rock, shell, or other meaningful earth element in your hand. If an emotion arises such as anger or sadness, feel it as you ask the Earth mother to ground or neutralize its energy into the object. Notice your body and your breath as you keep your attention focused on your connection with the earth. Allow the emotional energy to dissipate in its own time. When I feel melancholy I use this particular practice and find it to be peaceful, relaxing, and simultaneously energizing.

I'm becoming more cognizant of how bringing positive and

negative emotions and feelings into my conscious awareness is helping me to reconcile the fear and sadness that remains for me. Kevin recommended that I use Copaiba, an essential oil from the oleoresin of the Copaiba Tree that is known for helping the body to regulate its natural immune responses, lift spirits, and assist in emotional clearing. When I put four drops on my left foot for the recommended ten days, I felt its benefits. I also had greater trust in myself and my intuition.

The Mental Body

The emotional body is connected to the *mental body* and influences how we think, process information, solve problems, make judgments, express ourselves, and understand the world intellectually and analytically. The mental aspects of the self, solidified in positive and negative beliefs, are central to how thoughts create actions. Negative beliefs are based in trauma. In his work, Kevin has identified three negative belief structures that people seem to have to varying degrees. Stemming from past traumas, the mental body conjures a guiding belief that (1) 'It's not fair'; (2) 'I'm not good enough'; or (3) 'I am abandoned.' None of these statements is ever true in the total sense. I may not have been a good enough runner to win a race; this has nothing to do with being 'good enough' as a human being. Yet that experience of loss and perhaps the negative judgments from others, if not processed out of the body, can create an overarching subconscious belief of limited self-worth.

In Kevin's experience, all three of these belief structures

can be remediated by aligning with one's *source*. As a primary foundation, the source may be based in a moral code or a basic realization that we are each an integral part of a bigger system (such as a community, a religion, a nationality, a world). When people truly realize that they are connected, then they know without a doubt that their lives are inter-related to the lives of others. *Totalizing beliefs* that the world is not fair, that they are not good enough, or that they have been abandoned can no longer hold.

As a shamanic healer and transpersonal psychologist, Kevin identifies the primary negative belief structures at work in people's lives and teaches them how to diminish them through meditation and affirmation. The affirmations can be used to counter the negative belief structures that are lodged in the mental body.

For example, the first belief structure of 'It's not fair' had a major impact on my mental body. With the assistance of the pendulum swing, Kevin intuited that this negative structure constituted 90 percent of my mental body. It took up so much mental space that I had only 10 percent of it left to connect to my source. Intuitively, I knew it was an accurate read. I have always believed that the neglect and abuse of animals, women, children, and the environment is deeply flawed and unjust. I never considered that this belief could have a harmful impact on my psyche or my health. Yet viewing the world through the lens of unfairness took hold in a way that put me on constant alert and exacerbated my feelings of isolation. I functioned from a deep-seated belief that I was an island who could do it all without any help. It was stifling, yet it has always been a driving force in my life.

For more clarification about this belief structure, Kevin asked me to draw a Tarot card. I reached for the deck and drew the *two of pentacles*, a card that represents an ability to keep everything in balance. That was my lesson. It's not possible to have balance when being ruled by a totalizing belief in the inherent unfairness of the world. That negative thought pattern makes it difficult to remain open to new developments and go with the flow. To restructure the 'not fair' belief structure, one can assert a connection to the source and then observe the world as it truly is, both just and unjust. My affirmation was:

> "I can bring the suffering I see into my heart.
> I have the power to do this, knowing that all I
> experience is of God."

This enlightened perspective on how the world operates diminished the sadness and frustration I experienced in the face of injustice. It opened the possibility that I can be a witness to suffering and an advocate for its remediation in constructive ways, all without absorbing the heartache.

The second belief structure of being 'not good enough' was less significant for me. Despite my experiences of abuse, I had confidence in my skills and abilities, earned a solid education, built a professional career, managed my own businesses, traveled to new places, and brought everything to fruition that I've set my mind toward. I was highly functional and satisfied with my work and my choices in life. Had this belief structure been playing more of a role, I could have declared: "I am more than enough when connected to the Source." In truth, anyone would likely benefit from this affirmation.

The third overarching belief structure that can negatively take control of the mental body through trauma is that of 'abandonment.' It doesn't require being left on a doorstep as an infant for this belief to take hold, though desertion could certainly lead to such an imprint. When a child's needs for care, safety, self-esteem and other basics are not met, a core belief in abandonment can take root in the unconscious. Accepting this unconscious belief structure as an unchanging truth impacts how one relates to themselves and others as well as their vision of the world. Without knowing it, people may be predisposed to get involved with others who are physically or emotionally abusive and controlling. They might have a continuous suspicion that others will leave them or let them down. If this negative belief structure remains intact, it has the capacity to rule their life. To interrupt it, one could speak these words: "God presence and the oneness of all: I know I am that."

To break all negative belief structures, Kevin recommends making daily affirmations part of one's meditation. Since the body is more open to meditative practices when it is in a relaxed state, he suggests using essential oils to unwind and cut the edge of daily life. During my session, he suggested that I use coriander essential oil, which helps to elevate mood, calm nerves, and help with mental focus.

The Spiritual Body

> Awareness of the spiritual body is the most challenging aspect of this work for most people.
>
> *–Kevin Snow, the Desert Shaman*

The *spiritual body* involves a sense of connection to all things, including people, nature, the soul, what we call God, and all of life. It is the eternal path to expanded awareness and higher consciousness. When the physical, mental and emotional bodies are in balance, the higher vibrational energy of the spiritual body can be awakened to reveal one's spiritual nature. Some may call it the light of the soul. When thoughts of any kind invade the spiritual body, it can be very difficult to be aware of its existence at all. Thoughts activate beliefs which in turn elicit emotions that result in physical responses that distract the mind. Because consciousness works in this way, it can be a challenge to reach the expanded states of awareness that lead to enlightenment and the full expression of who we are as eternal beings.

In Kevin Snow's framework for harmonizing the four bodies, 80 percent of the spirit body would optimally be comprised of thoughts that are neutral, leaving space for an equal balance of positive and negative thoughts. Different from beliefs, thoughts are the notions that occur suddenly in the mind. For most people, these thoughts tend to fall on the negative side rather than simply being neutral. In fact, Kevin has found that the majority of people have a spirit body comprised of 80 percent negative thoughts.

I hate the humidity. People are stupid. Why is this line so long? That's an ugly dress. I need to mow the lawn. She's always mad at me. I can't figure this out. The floor is dirty. I have a headache. Ouch. I'm fat. I should take a walk.

The litany of thoughts is never ending, and these may or may not be fully formed expressions. Feelings, inklings, visions, impressions, musings, reflections, memories, colors, and so on, all count as thoughts. Whether positive or negative, forming attachments to those thoughts consciously or subconsciously rather than letting them flow through the mindscape, floods the spirit body and leaves little room for higher consciousness to be revealed. To release ourselves from an overabundance of positive or negative thoughts, we must create a spacious mind in which the light of consciousness may shine through.

In our session, Kevin intuited that my meditation and healing work has kept my spiritual body clear of negative thoughts. He told me he'd never seen such a clear spiritual body in any of his clients. He turned to another deck of Tarot cards called the 'Spirit of the Wheel.' This deck is used primarily to situate a person within the Medicine Wheel. The card drawn is like a stone in the wheel, a physical representation with a specific location. He drew the *Corn Planting Moon* (#21) card, which represents a particular time of year in Native American astrology that signals a time of great energy and enthusiasm.

In the light of this auspicious moon, the fears that once held a person back dissolve. It is said that "one can achieve great things by channeling this surge of creative energy and balancing it with clear direction."[17] I pray:

> "May I channel my energies in a healthy, positive, and balanced manner. And remember to be gentle with myself and others along the way."

I incorporated this prayer into my meditation practice right away. I'd sit and breathe for a few minutes, then say the prayer ten times: *The fears that held me back in the past dissolve in the light of this auspicious moon.* As I meditated on the meaning of the card, I'd monitor my body to observe whether my heart felt open or contracted. This practice made me more aware of how my beliefs on a given day affected my thoughts. Did I really believe that my fears would dissolve or was I just thinking it? This meditation and prayer helped me to identify the moments when my thinking mind was getting in the way of my connection with my source.

For additional guidance from the upper world, Kevin drew two more cards from the Tarot and Angel card decks. The *Three of Pentacles* represented creative work that earns a living. The *Archangel Michael* suggested that I am a powerful light worker, teacher, and healer. Kevin sensed my astonishment. When someone is surprised about a message that comes up in a session, it typically indicates that they need integration. How is it that my purpose is to teach and heal?

Although I have felt confident in and connected to my therapeutic work, I've never thought of myself as a 'powerful light worker.' What's more, it never occurred to me that the reason that I never considered my work as a Reiki healer or energy worker to be *light work* was that I didn't feel safe enough to be powerful in that way. When Kevin asked me to speak the words, "It is safe for me to be powerful" my chest and body tightened. Clearly, I was resistant to that statement. To release the fear that I had about owning up to myself as a powerful light worker, Kevin recommended the following daily affirmations:

"It is safe for me to be powerful."

"My spiritual power brings great blessings in loving service to the Divine."

"I am a powerful light worker."

To enhance my meditation and support my spiritual body further, I put Golden Rod essential oil on my forehead at the hairline, half-way between the third eye (also known as the 'inner eye,' a place of inner knowing) and the crown of my head. Kevin recommended that I do this for three weeks to help to quiet my mind and settle my body as I sat down to meditate. I have to admit that when I first started using the Golden Rod I felt a bit loopy. It only lasted for a few minutes until my body adjusted, and I felt noticeably calmer when I used it.

Ultimately, Kevin Snow sees the four bodies as a three-dimensional version of the soul. In other words, when these four bodies are in harmony they can give us a window into our Soul.

It Shall Be Written

At the end of that first private session with the Desert Shaman, he said one last thing: a surprising decree that changed the course of my life for over a year. He told me to write a book. "I have no idea what to write about," I quipped. "Write about the healing process from your childhood trauma up until now."

Events and turning points on my spiritual path flooded my brain. Eva, my sister traveler. Sedona. The Kogi. Mooji. Monte Sahaja. The birth of *Sanoja*. I blurted, "I can do that."

The medicine animal totem card I drew during that session came to mind: *Spider* –Mother of the Void, the original womb. The spider represents creativity communicated through writing. She spins the web that creates the first alphabet. Along with the *Hierophant* card that encouraged healing through the interpretation of life's mysteries and sacred truths, the message to write and publish a book was clear. Telling this story in a way that will resonate with others who are seeking liberation and recovery will be a healing gift.

Kevin was not the first person to suggest that I write a book, though I never truly considered it. As a doctor, I could discuss health and healing. As *Sanoja*, I could explore knowing and being my eternal Self. It didn't occur to me at the time that the writing of this story would force me to remember in great detail the trauma that set off a lifetime of profound and at times painful experiences. I'd have to relive it, think through it, feel it, acknowledge its effects on my body, my relationships, and my life.

I must have unconsciously agreed to the idea at some point along the way: My heart answered the call before my head could talk me out of it! Yet shortly after our session I started to wade through my memories of that day in the sandbox. Five-year-old Karen kicking up dust in her patent leather shoes before diving into a living room rumpus with her brothers and sister. The teenage boy next door who got off on molesting children. The secret despoiling of a little girl. The ravages of masculinity gone so wrong, it would take decades to unravel its deleterious effects and even longer to heal its wounds. The risk of vulnerability. Do I really want to do this?

It's not a matter of desire to share the intimate details of the trauma and abuse that stole part of my childhood and cast doubt on a young girl's sense of security about her place in the world. It's that my journey toward liberation demands it. Each memory and point on the scatterplot of my eternal trajectory breaks down some of the scar tissue left behind. The ritual and ceremony of writing and remembering unite with sacramental offerings, sacred pilgrimages, and everyday connections with something higher. They each add *meaning* to the wound, itself a curative property. As I craft this book, I sense my healing.

That being written, creation demands determination as much as faith, sensibility, and support. I made a promise to myself and to the Great Spirit within to tell this story. I'd need grit and help to see it through. Kevin, the Desert Shaman who safely interceded on my behalf has been an integral part of my healing. The next time I met with him, I sealed my commitment to this book with a Lakota prayer tie ceremony.

Invoking the Muse with a Lakota Prayer Tie Ceremony

Many indigenous peoples make and assemble prayer ties (sometimes called prayer flags) as offerings to the *Great Spirit*.

The ties are spiritual symbols made with a small square of cotton cloth in which tobacco (a sacred medicine) is placed and then tied with cloth or cotton string while praying and meditating. Traditionally, the ceremony ends with the burning of the ties, which sends the prayers to the heavens in clouds of smoke.

Prayer Ties from Ceremony

Before starting the ceremony, I created a *Medicine Wheel* in my backyard. Stone medicine wheels have been around for millennia and are based in a core principle of indigenous peoples around the globe: *Once you fully embrace the elemental forces of nature you become a part of the whole.*[18]

Medicine Wheel

As a symbol of symmetry and balance and a tool for introspection and healing, the medicine wheel is another way to engage with the interplay of the *physical, emotional, mental, and spiritual* aspects of ourselves. Thus, it is divided into the four quadrants to help people to recognize areas of their lives that need attention. Each direction and point around the perimeter represents a particular behavior or quality. If someone is lacking in that quality, it becomes their *medicine* as the person incorporates it into his or her life. To build my medicine wheel, I chose eight stones about one foot in diameter from my backyard. I placed each stone in the four cardinal directions and one between the cardinal directions to make a circle. The four points of a medicine wheel and its corresponding colors can be made to parallel the four bodies and qualities to promote their balance.

Figure 2: Elements of a Medicine Wheel

Direction	Color	Body Quadrant	Quality
North	White	Spirit	Wisdom
South	Red	Mental	Activation of New Energy
East	Yellow	Physical	Calling in New Energy
West	Blue	Emotional	Acceptance (letting go of attachments)

In addition to noting the directional aspects of the medicine wheel, Kevin drew cards from an Animal Totem deck. an animal would be assigned to each cardinal point to represent the qualities I want to invoke into my four bodies to create balance and promote self-healing.

The *Dolphin* card in the northern quadrant refers to the power of breath and sound. These great mammals enter the waters of life to call forth what is most needed or desired. The *Mountain Lion* of the southern quadrant represents leadership and the ability to respond to any situation with a balance of power, intention, strength, and grace. The *Antelope* of the western quadrant is a messenger of higher purpose that calls upon the mind's adaptability and capacity to respond quickly and take action. In the eastern quadrant, the *Grouse* stands for personal power and the 'sacred spiral'-- an ancient portrayal of universal energy that symbolizes the continuous cycles of growth, death, and rebirth. Similar to the spirals of fingerprints or the double helix of DNA, cosmic force reveals itself. In the practical realm, we begin to recognize patterns in our lives. Such awareness can serve as an indicator that we have moved beyond it. This is ascension to a higher level of consciousness.

With my medicine wheel ready, I prepared for the Lakota Tie Ceremony by bathing myself, my supplies and the wheel itself with sage smoke. *Smudging* as they call it entails burning a tightly bundled bunch of dried herbs (like sage) and diffusing the smoke into the ceremonial space to center oneself, purge negative energy, and purify personal articles.

Then I cut small squares of white, red, yellow and blue cotton fabric to make the ties. Within Lakota tradition, the colors of the cloth symbolize different prayers: *white* for healing, *red* for honoring ancestors, *yellow* for giving thanks, *blue* for letting go of attachments. I placed a pinch of rolling tobacco into the center of each square and transmitted my prayers into the tobacco medicine, folding each cloth several times before tying a red string around the bottom to lock it in place. Historically, red string is used to protect against negative energy. I continued four times until sixteen ties were sequenced by color down the string. Once complete, I wrapped the ties around a tree in my backyard adjacent to my medicine wheel.

I ended the ceremony with a Lakota Sioux prayer *Aho Mitakuye Oyasin* which means: 'I am related to everything.' I felt like I witnessed a rippling effect of personal healing on all of life.

Each individual, restored and in relationship with the whole, can do no harm. One person's healing is a salve for the world.

I sat in the medicine wheel to meditate daily, then stood next to the north stone with my hands lightly touching the prayer ties that were on the tree. I prayed to the *Great Spirit:* "May there be healing to all who want it, and may this life, in some way, be of benefit to all." I felt an expansion of being that reached well beyond my body and the tree every time I said the prayer. Physically touching the tree and the ties helped me to feel that expansion.

As time went on, squirrels ran up and down the tree and ended up breaking the string into pieces. I tied them back together. Despite my efforts, these lively creatures let me know that I, too, was sharing their space. After I found the ties on the ground for a third time, I decided to hold one more ceremony. At the end of it, I buried the ties in the earth beneath the North stone. All of the prayers held therein would become part of the sacred Earth, reverberating throughout, to support the healing of humankind.

Chapter 4

CULTURAL DENIAL OF ABUSE

When I was a child of abuse, I saw two ways to survive. Victimized or disconnected.

Victimization came with a sense of anger and resentment that felt out of character for me, but detachment gave me a way to get on with my life and regain control.

When I became cognizant of my past and the wound it left behind, I realized that I wasn't truly free. Fears and doubts lingered beneath the surface, trapping a resistant little girl within a grown woman's body.

To be liberated, I needed to tend to that old, festering wound. To allow the unconscious to be conscious. To be authentic and raw about who I really am.

I grew up in a fairly religious household. Every week my mother took my brothers, sister and me across town to an Episcopal church. It was tradition. We were all baptized there as infants and confirmed when we reached the 8th grade. For those unfamiliar with the sacrament of Confirmation, it is a mature reaffirmation of the baptismal rite that typically involves weeks of Bible study. We learned about Christian ministry and the Episcopal church and its structure. We memorized prayers and practiced sacraments, and ultimately affirmed our faith publicly by the laying on of our Bishop's hands.

Even without this faithful encouragement, I was curious about the Bible and started reading it on my own as a young adolescent. I liked the memorable stories. Nevertheless, I could barely keep up with the 46 parables of Jesus. I knew they were meant to speak to everyday people and teach moral lessons, still the manifold interpretations confused me.

The parable that Jesus told about the Good Samaritan in the book of Luke, for instance, made sense to me at first. It was about a traveler who had been attacked by thieves, beaten, stripped naked, and left to die along a road. The injured man was ignored by two passersby, first a priest and then a Levite (a Jewish man descended from the Tribe of Levi). They both crossed the street to avoid the man. Eventually, a Samaritan (known to be descended from the Israelites) came along and took pity on the poor soul. After dressing his wounds, the *good* Samaritan loaded the limp fellow onto his donkey and led him to an Inn where he paid the innkeeper to take care of him. It was a story of everyday compassion, of witnessing suffering and doing something to offer comfort. I could get behind that. All the same I wondered why the priest did nothing to help a stranger in need.

Our clergy never addressed what the priest should have done, and every time I heard a sermon about the good Samaritan it seemed to be told differently. The passersby didn't help because they thought that the scene was a trap set by robbers, or that the man was already dead and they would become *unclean* if they touched the body, or that helping someone on the street was beneath their social standing. I believed in a higher power and wanted to believe the words of Jesus. I wanted to believe that he spoke in parables to convey the spiritual essence of the Truth. Yet the seemingly endless interpretations of his stories didn't measure up. This left me wondering if I was some heathen who lacked the heart to understand God.

The last straw was when I heard a televangelist expound with thorough conviction that everyone should live in fear of God's wrath. The reason: we have all sinned, fallen short of His glory, and therefore, deserved punishment which would be swift and ongoing, if not eternal. This message was not appealing to a formerly abused girl struggling against victimhood.

I found solace in the knowledge that I wasn't the only person in the world to find some Christian teachings to be confusing. As one story goes, Jesus appeared to the great master Babaji, giving him the task of sending an emissary to the west to teach his followers how to *commune inwardly* with him in meditation. Jesus asked the saint to send someone to the West to remind his people that the goal of life is to become one with God through *inner communion.* The person Babaji found to share Jesus's message was Paramahansa Yogananda.

Born in 1893, Yogananda was the first yoga master of India to take up permanent residence in the West. A devotee of Jesus Christ, Yogananda introduced millions of westerners to the teachings of meditation and Kriya Yoga through his book *Autobiography of a Yogi.*[19] First published in 1946, the book chronicled his life and spiritual journey. He recounted his time living at an ashram, how he met his guru Swami Sri Yukteswar Giri and—with specificity, humor and humility—his direct experiences with God.

For example, in chapter 16 of the *Autobiography of a Yogi,* Yogananda comes to understand that only deep prayer and meditation allow human beings to connect with their divine consciousness and, in turn, to influence the universe through the subtle vibrations that arise from deep self-realization. A human being *is* an embodied soul after all. When a person truly realizes that identifying solely with thoughts or bodily experiences creates compulsive patterns such as addictions or feelings of lack that lead to aberrant behaviors or maladaptations, connecting with spirit offers inward protection that can mitigate these harmful effects. "The starry inscription at one's birth," Yogananda states, "is not that man is a puppet of his past. Its message is rather a prod to pride; the very heavens seek to arouse man's determination to be free from every limitation." Yogananda clearly views each human being as essential to the universal structure; a soul endowed with individualism and the personal will to find either liberation or enslavement. The choice in this moment and forever, is ours.

The insights and teachings of Yogananda's autobiography reinvigorated spiritual discipline with moving testimony that put all holy texts into an illuminating context. "Placing the holy texts on the spotless table of his mind, [Yogananda's Hindu guru] was able to dissect them with the scalpel of intuitive reasoning, and to separate errors and interpolations of scholars from the truths as originally expressed by the prophets."[20] The following conversation about the *Bhagavad Gita* aroused the guru's droll criticism.

> The stanza reads: "Fix one's vision on the end of the nose."
>
> The guru's remark: "The path of a yogi is singular enough as it is. Why counsel him that he must also make himself cross-eyed? The true meaning of *nasikagram* is 'origin of the nose,' not 'end of the nose.' The nose begins at the point between the two eyebrows, the seat of spiritual vision."

The image of millions of cross-eyed yogis makes me chuckle, as does the comical yet rational practicality of a renowned spiritual teacher. I marveled at what he might say about Biblical scriptures.

Yogananda admitted to his teacher that the story of Adam and Eve in the book of Genesis was incomprehensible to him [e.g., Why did God punish innocent unborn generations instead of only the 'guilty' pair?]. The guru explained the symbolism of the book. The human form (represented by Adam and

Eve) did not solely result from evolution; animal forms were too crude to express full divinity. In an act of creation, God made the human species by materializing human bodies and exclusively giving human beings tremendous mental capacity, as well as awakened energetic centers in the spine. *Reason* and *feeling* (as dualities, or polarities that underlie the phenomenal worlds) remain cooperative so long as the human mind is not tricked by its animal propensities. Knowledge of *good* and *evil*, a cosmic dualistic compulsion... facilitates every human being's innate desire to restore his dual nature to a unified harmony (represented by Eden).

Yogananda learned to understand and perceive the liberating knowledge of the Bible through Sri Yukteswar's wisdom and his capacity to move beyond literal interpretation. The dualities of reason and feeling show us that reason without feeling cultivates animalistic behaviors. For example, when reason overcomes the heart it opens the possibility of justifying difference, separation, inequality, and victimization. Although I struggled with religiosity for many years, I had new respect for the pages of Genesis and the Bible after reading the autobiography of this yogi. I knew with certainty that human understanding of the Divine originated from the heart. The mind's task was to organize it without thinking it into oblivion.

By the time I was around 30 years old, I came across a simple meditation book written by a U.S-based Indian spiritual teacher, Eknath Easwaran, which explained the role of meditation for spiritual growth.[21] All the would-be meditator had to do was choose an inspirational passage from any of the world's great religions, memorize it, and mindfully repeat it to oneself for 30 minutes every day. It sounded straight-forward, so I tried it. I had been exposed to Christianity for most of my life, so I chose the prayer of Saint Francis of Assisi to be my mantra.[22] Each morning, I sat quietly and silently recited the words.

> Lord, make me an instrument of your peace:
> Where there is hatred, let me sow love;
> where there is injury, pardon;
> where there is doubt, faith;
> where there is despair, hope;
> where there is darkness, light;
> where there is sadness, joy.
> O divine Master, grant that I may not so much seek
> to be consoled as to console,
> to be understood as to understand,
> to be loved as to love.
> For it is in giving that we receive,
> it is in pardoning that we are pardoned,
> and it is in dying that we are born to eternal life.
> Amen.

I felt at peace by the end of my half-hour of meditative prayer. After a while it seemed to echo within my being without my thinking or saying the words at all. This is how mantras and chanting work. Repeat the mantra over and over until your being resonates with its essence. When I started to think about the last verse of Saint Francis's prayer, my rational mind got skeptical.

Did the gentle saint mean to suggest that a person could only know God through physical death? Was I inadvertently praying for my own mortality? I did want to know God, but I wasn't ready to check out of my earthly existence.

Enlightenment came to me when I viewed the verse in the context of the rest of the prayer. It's all about non-dualism. Where there is darkness, there is light; in death, there is life. As Yogananda's guru reminded him that human beings must resist the instinctual tendencies that misinform, Saint Francis told me that everything is one. The individual soul is to be sublimated into the greater identity of the all-pervading One from whence it came. I used Saint Francis's prayer as a mantra meditation for many years after that.

The Upanishads

> Like two birds sitting on a tree branch: one is
> the small self that is doing and experiencing life;
> the other is the *witness* that does not partake, the
> eternal Self or soul.
>
> -- *The Upanishads* [23]

In the late 1980's, I was still searching for the truth of who I am. I went to the Eastern philosophies section of the bookstore to find other books from Eknath Easwaran who, in addition to being a spiritual teacher, had been a professor of Victorian literature. I loved his easy-to-understand meditation book and yearned to learn more from him. A book called *The Upanishads*[24], precariously positioned and almost falling off the shelf, called to me. Easwaran's translation of these ancient lyrical verses has become a core text for philosophy courses and anyone interested in Indian spirituality. The inside cover read:

> The *Upanishads* are a collection of texts written more than 5000 years ago...As others were exploring the external world, the Sages of India embarked on an extraordinary experiment turning inward to explore consciousness itself. In the changing flow of human thought, they asked, is there anything that remains the same? They found that there is indeed a changeless Reality underlying the ebb and flow of life.

This series of Hindu treatises focused on turning inward to explore consciousness. Its teachings offered me a pathway to access my eternal Self. I realized that a person's *essential nature* has no agenda with the mind, body, or world. It is pure awareness, like an empty space that wholly and intimately allows into existence whatever manifests within it. Like those two birds sitting on that tree branch, the small self is the one doing and experiencing life; the other self, the one who does not partake, is the eternal one – *the witness.*

From the perspective of a spiritual quest, *awareness* can be described as the *presence of that which is aware.* It is a quality of being, or being-ness, in which the Seer and the witness of the seeing are one and the same. Cultivating a sense of awareness in which a person experiences the world and observes that experience simultaneously is at the heart of this and many other spiritual practices. The words "be knowingly that" capture the essence of this teaching. As I practiced meditation, I too started to become more aware of myself as both the one who is experiencing life and witnessing it. I found a pathway to my eternal Self.

What I enjoyed most about reading Easwaran's translation of *The Upanishads* was how it helped me to see the esoteric and the everyday join together in a delightful way. Page by page, distinct levels of awareness came to me like *aha* moments from the seat of my stationary bicycle. That's right, it is possible to experience the 'Divine play' of life's illusions while pedaling 60 rpms and getting nowhere fast! I must have read the book a dozen times. Uplifted with a joy I'd never felt before, I saw a greater glimpse of that true essence of myself that does not change. The illusion that *is* life, revealed in subtle glory. I realized that enlightenment cannot be attained through religious creed or philosophy or membership in the 'right' organization. Inner awareness *necessarily* comes from within.

Losing My Religion

> The whole purpose of religion is to facilitate love and compassion, patience, tolerance, humility, and forgiveness.

> – *Dalai Lama XIV*

I'd had a spiritual connection throughout my life. Yet even when I found solace in prayer and verse, organized religion did not help my holy communion. I saw intolerance from members of the church, insincerity from religious leaders, people turning a blind eye to abuse, and murderous Crusades in the name of God. For thousands of years, a focus on the 'right' belief and the 'right' doctrine promoted a 'my way is the only way' mentality. If the *purpose of religion is to facilitate love, compassion, patience, tolerance, humility, and forgiveness* as the 14th Dalai Lama suggests, something went terribly wrong. In religion and elsewhere, there is division rather than unity, devotion toward ideas of individual redemption instead of acceptance that there are multiple ways of experiencing God.

Narrow conventions of truth spawn intolerance, injustice, subjugation and suffering, if not direct violence. I have experienced each of these: (1) as a 5-year-old girl pressed to the ground with no recourse but to agonize in silence until the vehement memory carved a deep plot within her embodied psyche; (2) as a teenage girl violated in the shelter of her own bedroom and forbidden from reporting the attack; (3) as a woman reaching for safe haven and understanding in a society structured to repudiate her assault and overlook her perpetrators; and (4) as a seeker of spiritual communion ready to embrace the universal consciousness from which all existence arises yet unable to situate that quest within the religious tradition that gave her the urge to know God in the first place. It's time to think differently. Religion has a role to play.

Devout Christian and former U.S. president Jimmy Carter

spoke repeatedly about religion and the use of scripture to promote various forms of violence, most acutely the discrimination and abuse of women and girls. In 2009, he wrote an open letter severing ties with the Southern Baptist Convention that he'd been a member of for six decades because he could no longer stand by while organizational leaders took scripture out of context to elevate men and boys through the suppression of women and girls.[25] In fact, the *Genesis* story that Yogananda found to be incomprehensible when taken literally, Carter saw as unfathomable in that it served as religious rhetoric to promote women's innate and Biblically mandated subservience to men. The biased conviction that women and girls must be the sullied and weaker sex functioned to condone their lesser access to basic human rights (health, education, employment, equal pay, and social influence included). In its most vile expression, this belief in women's and girls' lesser status excused violence, slavery, sexual abuse, and lack of control over their bodies and lives.

Carter makes a strong case for the dangers of taking scripture too literally. Indeed, women and girls have been paying the price for Eve's being tricked into eating that proverbial apple for thousands of years. Still, Genesis is the opening chapter of one of the most influential spiritual texts in existence. It must be of great import. Still, I'm not sure how to integrate its message into my relationship with spirit. The narrative goes something like this. The Devil takes the form of a talking snake that deceives the first woman on earth into eating a piece of fruit that she picked from the one forbidden tree in the Garden. She shares the fruit with the first man who ever lived, presumably her husband.

After eating it, the couple has a new-found awareness of good and evil, a perpetual war of dualism until the end of time. They soon find out that this knowledge comes at a high price. God casts them out of their heavenly abode here on earth, and they and their children must fend for themselves from that point on. Facing tremendous difficulties and pain, the first family and their descendants live out their human lives until they are dead and buried. Ultimately, God willing, they ascend to heaven.

A literal reading of the Adam and Eve story not only places the woman at fault for the fall of humanity, it separates human beings from their God-like natures when, according to the book of Luke, the kingdom of God is within. The explanation that resonates more with me comes from Sri Yukteswar, who explained its symbolism many years ago to his devout student Yogananda. The tree of life in the story actually represents the human body. The serpent symbolizes the body's energy as it coils through the spine. Sri Yukteswar clarified:

> The spinal cord is like an upturned tree, with man's hair as its roots, and ... nerves as branches. The tree of the nervous system bears many enjoyable fruits, or sensations of sight, sound, smell, taste, and touch. In these, [human beings] may rightfully indulge; but [they were] forbidden the experience of sex, the 'apple' at the center of the bodily garden.[26]

From Yukteswar's perspective, sex represents instinct-bound (i.e., animalistic) drives too crude to express full divinity. As reason ('need') and emotion ('desire') come together to make up the totality of human experience, human beings have the task of rising above their instinctual energies to reach God. This instinctual drive correlates with what we now know about the reptilian brain. Consisting of the upper part of the spinal cord and the basal ganglia, the reptilian brain is triggered by fear, gratification, and power.

Sri Yukteswar argued that moving beyond the animalistic is essential for feeling love, compassion, patience, tolerance, humility, and forgiveness. It is also vital for realizing higher consciousness. This deeper understanding of human beings' innate drive toward spiritual communion is demonstrated across religious traditions and before the birth Christ. Others believe that the apple represents the knowing of our true eternal Selves as we live in the dualistic world of good and evil.

Jimmy Carter's life and political career have always had a strong humanitarian focus. He argued convincingly in his book, *A Call to Action: Women, Religion, Violence, and Power*, that discrimination against women and girls is "the most serious, pervasive, and ignored violation of basic human rights.[27] Carter shared his insights into what he calls a "global scourge of gender abuse" throughout the book, beginning with an address he made in 2009 to the Parliament of the World's Religions. He writes:

> I reminded the audience that in dealing with
> each other, we are guided by international

agreements as well as our own moral values, most often derived from the Universal Declaration of Human Rights, the Bible, the Koran, and other cherished texts that proclaim a commitment to justice and mercy, equality of treatment between men and women, and a duty to alleviate suffering.

However, some selected scriptures are interpreted, almost exclusively by powerful male leaders within the Christian, Jewish, Muslim, Hindu, Buddhist, and other faiths, to proclaim the lower status of women and girls.

This claim that women are inferior before God spreads to the secular world to justify gross and sustained acts of discrimination and violence against them. This includes unpunished rape and other sexual abuse, infanticide of newborn girls and abortion of female fetuses, a worldwide trafficking in women and girls, and so-called honor killings of innocent women who are raped, as well as the less violent but harmful practices of lower pay and fewer promotions for women and greater political advantages for men.

I mentioned some notable achievements of women despite these handicaps and described struggles within my own religious faith.

I called on believers, whether Protestant, Catholic, Coptic, Jew, Muslim, Buddhist, Hindu, or tribal, to study these violations of our basic moral values and to take corrective action.[28]

Carter sees religious leaders and believers as central to challenging the acceptance and propagation of gender oppression. There are increasing numbers of religiously-minded advocates who agree. Muslim women around the world who are scholars, teachers, and leaders of their religion have been organizing for gender equality and women's inclusion at all levels of the church. The global Muslim women's network, for example, focuses on mutual respect and kindness, particularly between spouses.[29] In opposition to the belief among some Muslims that the Quran allows husbands to strike disobedient wives, these and many other religious women leaders are working for more progressive and compassionate interpretations of scripture.

Unfortunately, violence and male dominance have become so normalized in our homes, communities, college campuses, law enforcement, the military, foreign policy, and in the culture at large that this deeply engrained problem will require broad-based action. Indeed, the roots of violence run deep through the traumas of everyday life.

For instance, former Penn State assistant football coach, Jerry Sandusky, was convicted of sexually abusing ten boys while working with several children's charitable organizations. His behaviors, however, were not isolated from the family setting. One of his sons, Matt Sandusky, felt like he had been groomed for sexual abuse by his father since he was in elementary school and through his teens. He has since committed himself to helping others who have been in a similar situation. He and his wife founded the Peaceful Hearts Foundation to help sexual abuse survivors. He believes that communities must confront and speak openly about sexual abuse if it is ever to end. Another son, Jeffrey Sandusky, took a different path. He was a steadfast defender of his father throughout the trial and conviction. More recently, he himself was charged with child sexual solicitation.[30] There are countless examples of abuse within families and communities.

Roots of Trauma and Abuse

> We do not arrive in this world as a clean slate. Every new baby comes with a history of its own, the history of the nine months between conception and birth. In addition, children have the genetic blueprint they inherit from their parents. These factors may help determine what kind of a temperament a child will have, what inclinations, gifts and predispositions.

> But character depends crucially upon whether a person is given love, protection, tenderness and understanding or exposed to rejection, coldness, indifference and cruelty in the early formative years. The stimulus indispensable for developing the capacity for empathy, say, is the experience of loving care. In the absence of such care, when a

child is forced to grow up neglected, emotionally
starved and subjected to physical abuse, he or she
will forfeit this innate capacity.

--Alice Miller, Ph.D. (1923–2010) [31]

Swiss psychologist and childhood development researcher
Alice Miller authored thirteen critically acclaimed books
translated into thirty languages. These writings focused
primarily on the impact of child abuse, punishment, and family
dysfunction on both the abused children and on the society
at large. In her first book, *The Drama of the Gifted Child*,[32] she
argued that all children endure trauma and lasting psychological
damage from parents who stringently impose codes of conduct.
Originally titled "Prisoners of Childhood," Miller made the case
that these parents tend to enforce their behavioral standards with
emotional manipulation and physical abuse. Abusive behaviors
can run the gamut of neglect, betrayal, mockery, humiliation,
spankings, slaps, beatings or, in some cases, sexual exploitation or
prolonged physical abuse. Although these actions cause harm to
a person's integrity and self-worth, Miller contends that children
assimilate and sometimes justify their abuse. They may believe
that they somehow deserved it, or they may completely repress
their memories.

Miller maintained that injured children, unable to defend
themselves or acknowledge the anger they rightly feel toward
their oppressors, results in unresolved traumas that become
imprinted into their psyches. This contributes to feelings of

self-doubt, perfectionism, mental illness, addiction, crime, or the abuse of others including their own children. Without acknowledgement and emotional resolution of childhood traumas, adults may suppress the resultant pain and anger only to cast it, if inadvertently, onto themselves and others.

Miller took her theory of childhood development further in her next two books, *For Your Own Good* (1983) and *Thou Shalt Not Be Aware* (1984). She posited that the ways in which families and societies condition children can have deleterious effects on their well-being and capacity to be fully functioning, empathetic adults. Those same parenting methods can produce generations of adults who are unable to question or challenge authority. Therefore, the atrocities of WWII, for example, were permitted to happen. She emphasized how the authoritarian childrearing methods created fertile ground for producing adults with exceptional abilities. These methods also created the likes of fanatical dictator Adolf Hitler and serial killer of young boys Jürgen Bartsch, two men with a profound predilection for extreme brutality.

Adolf Hitler's 1925 autobiographical book *Mein Kampf* (*My Struggle*)[33] does not paint a vivid picture of the heinous crimes he orchestrated. Yet his writings about how he became increasingly anti-Semitic and militaristic shed light on the man's violent disposition and the rationale behind his political ideology. The following excerpt is from the first section of Hitler's chapter on "Nation and Race."

> Any crossing of two beings not at exactly the
> same level produces a medium between the level

of the two parents. This means: the offspring will probably stand higher than the racially lower parent, but not as high as the higher one. Consequently, it will later succumb in the struggle against the higher level. Such mating is contrary to the will of Nature for a higher breeding of all life. The precondition for this does not lie in associating superior and inferior, but in the total victory of the former. The stronger must dominate and not blend with the weaker, thus sacrificing his own greatness. Only the born weakling can view this as cruel, but he after all is only a weak and limited man; for if this law did not prevail, any conceivable higher development of organic living beings would be unthinkable.

The consequence of this racial purity, universally valid in Nature, is not only the sharp outward delimitation of the various races, but their uniform character in themselves. The fox is always a fox, the goose a goose, the tiger a tiger, etc., and the difference can lie at most in the varying measure of force, strength, intelligence, dexterity, endurance, etc., of the individual specimens. But you will never find a fox who in his inner attitude might, for example, show humanitarian tendencies toward geese, as similarly there is no cat with a friendly inclination toward mice.

....

> And struggle is always a means for improving
> a species' health and power of resistance and,
> therefore, a cause of its higher development.

Despite Hitler's openly anti-Christian beliefs, what he describes here is the *Genesis* story all over again. Only in Hitler's version Adam is the *Aryan race*, Eve is the *inferior Jew*, and God is *natural law*. The logic is the same: codify the alleged superiority of one group over another to justify their subjugation and, in this case, complete annihilation. This reasoning propelled the existence of the racist tyrannical leader who organized the systematic gassings, shootings, death marches and starvation of millions of Jewish people. In some ways, it serves, too, as justification for the despicable horrors of Jürgen Bartsch. His was the first German case to introduce psycho-social factors as causal mechanisms of abusive and violent behavior of vulnerable children.

Alice Miller shared a portrait of Jürgen Bartsch to exhibit the *indescribable* cruelty of this disturbed young man.[34] The detailed descriptions that he gave during preliminary questioning and the trial revealed that his heinous acts were an outward expression of a lifetime of abuse that he experienced from an early age. Forbidden to play with other children because they might get him dirty, his grandmother locked him in a cellar with barred windows, ten-foot walls, and artificial light until he was old enough to go to school. When he was twelve, his parents enrolled him in a Catholic boarding school where he suffered humiliations, spankings, and sexual abuse. Violence, abuse, and isolation were fundamental to this young man's socialization.

Numerous accounts of Adolf Hitler's life describe a comfortable though discordant middle-class existence. Ian Kershaw's detailed descriptions of the Fuhrer's early life in his book *Hubris* [35] paint a picture:

> Adolf's early years were spent under the smothering protectiveness of an over-anxious mother dominated by the threatening presence of a disciplinarian father... Adolf's younger sister...spoke... of her mother as a 'soft and tender person, the compensatory element between the almost too harsh father and the very lively children who were perhaps somewhat difficult to train.... 'It was especially my brother Adolf who challenged my father to extreme harshness and who got his sound thrashing every day ... How often ...did my mother caress him and try to obtain with her kindness what the father could not succeed [in obtaining] with harshness!'

> Hitler himself, during his late-night fireside monologues in the 1940s, often recounted that his father had sudden bursts of temper... He did not love his father, he said, but instead feared him all the more.

It's not much of a leap to surmise that the roots of Adolf Hitler's tremendous hatred, brutality, thirst for dominance, and inability to develop deep personal relationships were seeded by his family circumstances – a child subjected to the thrashings and whims of a violent, domineering patriarch, and a maternal shield that could offer love without safeguard. Likewise, it's not so surprising in hindsight that the omnipresent butcher knife that threatened Jürgen Bartsch's corporeal existence became his tool of choice when attempting to gain a semblance of control over his ghastly life by turning on other vulnerable children.

And yet, *what could make such monsters out of these two men of humble and innocent beginnings?* This is the question Alice Miller explores in the context of the traditional childrearing ethos of Germany in the 19th and early 20th centuries, an era of *poisonous pedagogy* in which "physical abuse and humiliation produce unhappy and confused children which leads to a confused and irrationally functioning society."[36]

Miller adapted the concept of poisonous pedagogy – first introduced to describe physical and psychological violence within educational processes – to represent a repressive and harmful style of traditional child-rearing in the 19th and early 20th centuries in Germany in which parents used manipulative and coercive behaviors and interactions to *break the will of the child.* A series of parenting manuals by Dr. Daniel Schreber popularized the philosophy in the mid-1800s. He advised gaining mastery over a child beginning in infancy by withholding affection and using techniques such as "frightening" babies in an effort to stop their crying.[37] As children developed, parents were to quell any signs of willfulness, disobedience, or exuberance.

According to Miller, the religious values in Germany of the period encouraged beating children into submission as a kind of conditioning that called upon believers to recognize their *fallen natures* and take action to appease an angry and punitive God. Honoring thy father and mother especially by offering absolute deference to the patriarch of the family was synonymous with obeying the Heavenly father. Miller emphasized that some of the tortured children, like the Jürgen Bartsches and Adolf Hitlers of the world, would undoubtedly end up inflicting their childhood traumas on others to a horrifying degree. Given their circumstances, she says, it would almost be surprising if they didn't.

As Miller contends, children deprived of love and care can lose their capacity for love and empathy along with their ability to form reciprocal, mutually enhancing relationships such that violent adult behavior can represent unresolved childhood trauma. That said, childhood circumstances alone, no matter how inadequate or cruel, are insufficient to explain a young boy's rise to sadism or tyranny. Social and cultural factors create conditions that deter or promote violence, exploitation, and other abuses of power.

When explaining Hitler's rise to power and the tacit acceptance of Nazi control on the part of the German populace, Miller sums it up in terms of obedience and the suppression of personal will, deeply ingrained since childhood. Indoctrinated to accept orders and suppress any feelings or concerns about their potentially damaging or catastrophic effects, the German masses carried out their directives knowing that any challenge to the hierarchy would be met with egregious penalties. In addition to government mandated membership in the Nazi regime, Security Police crushed political opposition by force, arresting and killing civilians, civil servants, diplomats, and military officers who were noncompliant. As the self-aggrandized leader of Nazi dominion, Miller speculates that Hitler's belief system and dictates were a 'reenactment' of his childhood traumas. Instead of cast as the powerless child, he plays the role of the vengeful father with the German masses as his dutiful offspring. Hitler's experiences of extreme emotional and physical abuse in childhood along with his combat service resulted in severe psychiatric disorders and an extreme vulnerability to shame.

About 60 percent of men and 50 percent of women experience at least one trauma in their lives. Women are more likely to experience sexual assault and child sexual abuse, and men more typically experience traumas associated with physical assault, combat, disaster, or witness to death or injury.[38] Clearly, the lines of trauma overlap. Vietnam War veterans suffered some of the highest levels of psychological damage from their combat-related trauma. It is estimated that about 30 percent of Vietnam vets have had Post-Traumatic Stress Disorder (PTSD) in their lifetime. About 11 to 20 percent of those serving in Iraq and about 12 percent of Gulf War veterans, have had PTSD in a given year.

The stressors in combat are many: being at risk for death or injury; being shot at, attacked, or ambushed; knowing someone who was killed or seriously injured; having to be on constant alert; being away from family and friends; not always knowing when the tour of duty will end; killing or injuring others. In addition, about 55 percent of women and 23 percent of men report being sexual assaulted while in military service. Without addressing the emotional impacts of trauma, these veterans are at risk for PTSD, depression, and other mental health problems. Such factors contribute to difficulties when reintegrating into their post-duty lives including addictions, conflicts with others, suicide, and violent behaviors sometimes many years after returning from the battlefield.[39]

Socialization in the military, in schools, in sports, at home and elsewhere encourages people to keep their traumas and those they witness to themselves. Bullying and hazing are all too common examples. Bullying is intended to cause harm and is repeated over time whereas hazing is often viewed as a rite of passage that helps to build confidence, self-esteem, meaningful relationships within peer groups. Both are forms of violence that rely on an imbalance of power and encourage physical, verbal, and social abuse. More than 1.5 million high school students are hazed each year and 55 percent of college students involved in clubs, teams and organizations experience hazing. Although hazing leads to an alarming number of injuries, sexual assaults, and deaths each year, most incidents go unreported.[40]

Similarly, research shows that women and girls underreport sexual harassment and abuse.[41] The Association of American Universities' Campus Climate Survey of 27 universities found that 23 percent of undergraduate women and 5 percent of men experienced a range of abuses from sexual harassment to stalking, intimate partner violence, and rape. These were the students who completed the survey. On average, one in four women experience sexual assault while in college.[42] One of the barriers to reporting is that the procedures for adjudicating complaints vary widely across campuses and typically do not involve outside enforcement. School hearings operate outside of the criminal justice system, and many universities prefer to handle them in-house to avoid bad press and the risk of losing donors, enrollment, and programs.

In addition to the normalization of sexual assault and violence against women, girls fear retaliation and run the risk of not being believed, or being held responsible for the vicious behaviors of their perpetrators. One of the Catholic Church's high-ranking clerics, Cardinal Raymond Burke, claims that women themselves are to blame for the crisis of pedophile priests. He argues that serving mass is a 'manly' job, and that women have openly discouraged men from participating. The mere contribution of women and girls into the daily life of the church, such as introducing altar girls, changes the dynamic between priests and altar boys. This presence of girls and women, he says, has a chilling effect that causes priests to turn to 'immoral and unpriestly vocations' such as 'abusing minors'.[43]

Even when people know abusive behaviors are happening, they remain quiet largely due to an unwritten code of silence on the part of the victims and any witnesses. Children learn at a young age that tattling is unacceptable. In a recent editorial in the *Washington Post* about the latest string of hazing injuries and fatalities, Afshan Jafar, associate professor of sociology at

Connecticut College, explains how we socialize children not to resist peer pressure. She tells the story of a 5-year-old girl who went to a teacher on the playground to report that one of her classmates was screaming in fear and about to be shoved off of the sliding board. The teacher told the child to mind her own business and followed up with the suggestion that the classmate in question should also mind his. The little girl was confused. She feared for the boy and wanted to help. She enacted the role of the good Samaritan and believed this was the right thing to do. After being shamed by the teacher, she learned the lesson that speaking up and risking getting someone else into trouble, regardless of what they did or the harm it caused, is wrong. The following year, the teacher's assistant reaffirmed the message by instituting a "tattle report" for the 6-year-olds to fill out whenever they had a complaint. In it, they were required to list three nice things about the person they were "tattling" on before lodging their grievance.

I learned this lesson too when I was little. I remember a boy in my first-grade class who hit me across my face with his hat. When I got home and asked my mother why someone would do that, she said, "That's the way some people are." The next day, she came by the school to tell the teacher about it. When confronted, my classmate lied and blamed me for the altercation. Then he told everyone that I tattled even though I didn't. I never would have thought to tell the teacher in front of my classmates. I just asked my mother an innocent question. If we learn not to speak up when we experience or witness wrongdoing, is it any wonder that I never told anyone about the sexual assaults of my youth until well into adulthood?

In addition to being socialized to hide abuses and feel shame when calling them out, ordinary childhood experience can be damaging to one's sense of self. Alice Miller's ice-cream story is a good example.

> A two-year-old boy walking with his parents whined and cried for an ice-cream bar like the ones his parents were eating and enjoying. His parents each offered him a bite, but he didn't want it. He wanted an ice-cream bar of his own. He cried, and his parents laughed at all the fuss as they walked on.

> The child protested briefly, sitting on the ground and flinging stones over his shoulder, but quickly became anxious about being left behind. He got up and joined his parents, who were still both enjoying their treats. The more the boy cried, the more it seemed to amuse his parents.

> When the boy's father finished his ice cream, he offered the empty stick to his son and kept walking. The boy licked the bit of wood, looked at the stick and threw it aside. He sobbed briefly before trotting on obediently after his parents.

> -- *Summarized from Prisoners of Childhood* [44]

Miller explains that the boy's well-meaning parents were not cold or uncaring. They simply did not understand that what was at issue for the boy had nothing to do with the ice-cream bar. He just wanted to be included and respected. There's no way to anticipate how the boy will integrate this minor infringement into his sense of self. Miller suggests that such scenes tend to be replayed as children learn to break through feelings of their own helplessness by learning to contempt those who are smaller and weaker. The boys' parents, Miller argues, were very likely to be replaying some version of the ice-cream story themselves.

Both minor and major infringements can produce psychological difficulties that, if left unattended, can lead to ongoing problems that negatively impact health, relationships, and quality of life in adulthood. In addition to physical and sexual abuse, neglect, growing up with a depressed or alcoholic parent, living with divorce, being belittled or unsupported by the family, feeling isolated, all increase the chances of negative health effects and depression in adulthood. A landmark (1996) study of the associations between adverse childhood experiences and adult health risk behaviors and disease found a strong relationship between the breadth of exposure and multiple risk factors for smoking, alcohol or drug use, risky sexual behaviors and several of the leading causes of death in adults (including ischemic heart disease, cancer, chronic lung disease, skeletal fractures, and liver disease).[45] Numerous studies have replicated these findings.

Figure 3: Adverse Childhood Experiences (ACEs) are strongly related to the development and prevalence of a wide range of mental and physical problems throughout a person's lifespan.

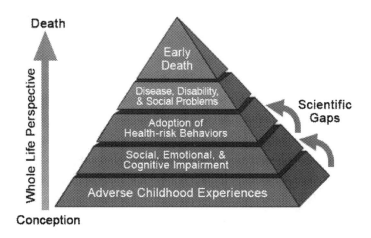

This graphic is used courtesy of the Substance Abuse and Mental Health Services Administration (SAMHSA), U.S. Department of Health and Human Services (HHS). Use of this graphic does not constitute or imply endorsement by SAMHSA or HHS of content or opinions in this book.

In addition to the personal and interpersonal outcomes of traumatic experiences, the most recent study of the *economic* burden of child maltreatment alone in the United States found that the total lifetime estimated financial costs associated with just one year of confirmed cases of child maltreatment (physical abuse, sexual abuse, psychological abuse and neglect) was approximately $124 billion, with the total burden estimated to be as large as $585 billion.[46] That data was from 2008.

Burying, and Unearthing Trauma

> The family and society perpetuate abuse by making everything a shameful secret. This makes it almost impossible for the abused to heal. There is such powerful yet unconscious emotion related to trauma, that the hidden wound festers and essentially runs their lives.

It was only recently that I reflected back on that day when I was 5 years old and my father stood next to my bed to remove the catheter that remained in my body following the severe bladder infection I acquired subsequent to Johnny's reprehensible, predatory escapades in his back yard. I can still see Dad's trembling hands, and mom holding back tears as she watched from the opposite side of my bed. There I was in the midst of this appalling scene without any understanding of rape or what had happened to me, why I was sick, or why my father was tending to my private parts as my mother stood by, a reticent witness to my pain and humiliation.

Once the catheter was removed, Dad tenderly pulled the sheets back up over me and kissed my cheek. A look of innocent, loving anguish cascaded across his face. Mom tucked the edges in behind my shoulders so as to reassure her little one that she was safe. Dad flipped off the light as they went out. "Get some rest," he said. Save for the languid rise and fall of worn cotton across my ribcage as I breathed, I lay in perfect stillness. Cocooned in my room, I knew they were ashamed.

By the time that I awoke the next day, I really had to pee. I threw off the covers and scuttled over to the bathroom. My stomach growled at the smell of toast wafting down the hallway. I'd already buried the details of the catheter removal, most likely somewhere near the trauma itself. My parents never discussed it. It wasn't until well into the writing of this book that this memory resurfaced in all of its horrific glory.

The recollection of that day flashed into my consciousness when I was at a meeting at work. Without warning my father's shame wrapped around me like a blanket. He didn't protect me from the child abuser next door. He'd failed. Tending to the innocent little girl's lower anatomy under the gaze of the woman who birthed her was an ironic atonement that intensified his disgrace. My throat tightened. I choked back tears. I felt my father's shame consciously for the first time. I realized in that moment that I had felt it and internalized it as my own. My office wasn't the place to work through the surfacing of a subconscious trauma. I acknowledged the feeling in my body and its relationship to that shameful series of traumatic experiences, promising myself to return to it when I got home. I would be the parent of the wounded child.

I walked home immediately after the meeting. In the sanctity of my personal space, my throat tightened again. I softened my breath, inhaling and exhaling slowly and deeply until my throat opened into an expanse of tears that shook me from my gut. I could feel the anesthetizing shame of a father who couldn't keep his vulnerable daughter safe and a little girl who never really trusted anyone after that. I was loved yet alone, left out of the closer-knit relationship he had with my brothers. I was insignificant, and he was powerless. I sobbed for an hour, emotions so raw that I broke through the knot of my own and my father's shame. Released from my body and soul after more than five decades, I was finally free. I had a choice in the matter. I felt unconditional love for my dad.

It's not surprising that it took me most of my life to begin to heal the traumas I experienced at a young age and then replayed as I moved through adulthood. Shame is so painful that people develop countless conscious and unconscious ways to cope. In fact, a common denominator in Alice Miller's writings on trauma and child abuse is that people subdue their victimization during childhood to avoid the unbearable pain of it. In other words, the suppression of trauma is a survival mechanism. Miller writes:

> It is true that our memories are unreliable, easily manipulated from within (our 'wishful thinking') and without. But above all they serve our will for survival. Our will for survival will never push us to invent painful stories, rather to the contrary: to make up nice memories in order to help obscure the painful reality of our childhood. The commandment that says 'Thou shalt not be aware of what was done to thee, nor of what thou doest to others' ensures that cruelty suffered in childhood is played down or modified by memory until it becomes unrecognizable.[47]

The *unconscious* choice to repress traumatic memories and remain *unaware* of those experiences can lead the abused person to displace resultant fear, shame, and pain and *redirect* it against themselves or others (through addiction, mental health problems, delinquency, interpersonal difficulties, negative consequences for work and family, or even violence and exploitation). Miller argues that it is the 'embodied memory' of trauma along with its emotional dimensions that triggers the compulsion to repeat that which was endured but not consciously remembered.

When I finally became conscious of the abuses I experienced as a child and adolescent, I took steps to process the abuse. Therapy sessions. Creative outlets. Theoretical frameworks. Intellectual musings. Heart-to-heart conversations. It wasn't until I *felt* the lingering effects of the trauma in my subtle body that I could truly acknowledge them and begin to heal. From this experience, I found that the key to healing from trauma is awareness of presence, which allows a knowing of who we truly are—Eternal.

Creating a Conscious Society

> It is not possible to address...the human and civil rights struggle of our time without looking at factors that encourage the acceptance of violence in our society.
>
> *Jimmy Carter, author of A Call to Action* [48]

When Jimmy Carter called upon society to stand up to moral violations that contribute to or directly cause suffering, he stood firmly against both the explicit and tacit acceptance of violence. This means that social institutions from the religious to the educational to the political to the familial (and beyond) must identify and castoff the roots of all violence, abuse, and injustice.

I agree with the former U.S. president's message. Efforts such as Doctors Without Borders, the United Nations' Global Partnership to End Violence Against Children, the Convention on the Elimination of All Forms of Discrimination Against Women (CEDAW), and the many other policies, programs, and initiatives currently underway to end violence and oppression while simultaneously helping to alleviate suffering are vital. I also believe that ending violence involves more than political will. It requires a major shift in consciousness.

The strongest foundation for empathy and compassion is the basic understanding that we're all in this life together.

Harm to the little girl is harm to myself.

Harm to the spouse is harm to myself.

Harm to the earth is harm to myself.

The oppression of one to elevate another is harm to the self.

Harm to the self, is harm to the whole.

Once I made the decision to seek the truth of who I am, I understood that my personal quest was really a universal one. Just as the seekers of past and present looked inward to find the eternal oneness of life, I too needed to seek the truth of who I am by seeking the Truth of the whole. I could no longer accept that one person's 'enlightenment' could come at the expense of

Chapter 5

WHO DO I THINK I AM?

...To praise that which is exalted...the divine.

-- On the meaning of kirtan, by
kirtan artist David Newman

My quest to know the truth about who I am started long ago and, as you might guess, I'm not one to leave any stone unturned to find out. In the earlier days of this ongoing journey, I drove about 30 minutes from where I lived to an ashram in Denton, TX, to turn a stone called *kirtan* – a call-and-response style mantra set to music. From the Sanskrit root meaning "to cut through," this practice is meant to cut through the idea of separation and connect, through sound, to the present moment, our hearts, each other, and the divine.[50] I loved the chants, the music, the feeling of unity, and that we didn't need a temple or church to create something sacred. I could join the blessed chorus on YouTube if I wanted, any time of day or night.

One of my favorite kirtan artists at the time was

Grammy-nominated vocalist Krishna Das. Known for his Hindu devotional music, Das engages in spiritual practices that cultivate love and devotion toward God (the universal, the divine). I listened to many of his recordings. My favorite, *Om Namah Shivaya*. The mantra means: "I bow to the Soul of all. I bow to you, Shiva, my own true Self, consciousness." In Hindu philosophy, Shiva is the destroyer of ignorance; namely the illusion of individuality. That nondual understanding that everything and everyone share the same essence continues to resonate with me.

I played and sang the mantra *Om Namah Shivaya* over and over again every night while I was cooking, until it was part of me. I'd wake up the next morning and feel the song playing in my heart. I didn't have to think the words or hum the tune. It was just there, reverberant. The mantra echoed throughout the day, filling me up with such devotion to God.

One night when I was listening to the mantra, a voice from within me said, "You must give up who you think you are." I resisted what I heard even though I didn't know what it meant. I thought about it. Why would I need to give up who I think I am? Life is good. I love my family and friends. I enjoy my work and am in service to my patients.

Then it dawned on me. All of those objects of desire are about Karen, an individual limited by body and mind. I yearned to know my eternal Self, the one that is infinite, that lacks nothing, that is one with everything and everyone. I know I am *that*.

I committed myself that moment to discovering the emptiness in all conceptions of 'Who I am.'

Taking Refuge in Buddhism

Giving up the ego is easier said than done. The mind gets carried away with likes and dislikes, memories and desires, reasons and justifications, lists of things to do and stuff left undone, and streams of thoughts to create and fortify a sense of 'Who I am.' It's all very exciting to the ego! It's also exhausting. The ego can never have enough, or be enough. Constantly craving, ego-consciousness doesn't know how to *be*. It is so powerful in creating an illusion of identity that the True Self, the eternal Self can be hard to find. Our true nature is empty of form yet everything we experience is its manifestation. It is no-thing and at the same time the source of everything — how do you wrap a mind around that? You can't. For this reason, the Buddha called the ego the *cause of all suffering*.

I resonate with the core teachings of the major religions. At this point in my journey, however, I was drawn to Buddhism and specifically the Buddhist perception of *emptiness*, which is a way of looking at the whole of experience not just what's front and center at any given time. Beliefs can and do change, even strong ones. A Catholic can become Protestant, or Buddhist. A Muslim can convert to Christianity and vice versa. Within organized religions, great reformations have occurred that fundamentally change core tenets of religious beliefs and practices. I wanted to know that which is eternal and unchanging. Discovering the nature of emptiness was the closest thing to eternal being I could find, so I went with it.

My relationship with Buddhism deepened with the venerable

Lama Dudjom Dorjee. He is a teacher in the Kagyu order of Tibetan Buddhism in residence at the Karma Thegsum Choling (KTC) Dallas meditation center, about 45 minutes from where I live. This highly-distinguished representative of one of Tibet's oldest and most sacred lineages studied Buddhist philosophy at Sanskrit University in Varanasi, India, where he and his family lived following the Chinese Communist invasion of Tibet. He earned the equivalent of a western Master's degree, authored seven books, and has been teaching in the west since 1982. I met him in 2011 after moving next door to one of his students.

My neighbor, Dawa, studied with Lama Dorjee for years and frequently invited him to give talks and retreats at the Dawa Dolma Meditation Center that she runs. We talked about Buddhist teachings often over tea, and I wanted to learn more about how Buddha found freedom. Although different schools of Buddhism have distinctive views about who the Buddha was, there is agreement that Buddhism exists to address the problem of *suffering*, caused by the ego. Then, we come to recognize that this suffering is noble because it is the starting point of, and inspiration for, taking a spiritual path. Living mindfully and practicing meditation to dissolve the ego cultivates wisdom and truth, ultimately ending that suffering. This is 'enlightenment' and is called 'nirvana' in Tibetan Buddhism. But how did he do it? When Lama Dorjee gave Dawa the go-ahead to teach an "Introduction to Buddhism" class a few months later, I was the first to sign up.

I learned that Buddhism is not about salvation or original sin or becoming somebody different. It's about the basic goodness of all beings. This reminds me of the prayer of Saint Francis that I so dearly love and by which I model my life. In Tibetan Buddhism, Buddha was not a God, a deity, or divine being. He was an ordinary person with purely human faculties who discovered the path to awakening. Anyone can follow this path to the same enlightenment. There is no savior. It's up to us to search within and discover. Even when Buddhists take refuge in Buddha, we are really taking refuge in our own true nature; sometimes called Buddha nature, ordinary mind, Vajradhara, or just plain Buddha: 'Awake.'

After studying Buddhism with Dawa and reflecting on what the teachings mean for the human condition, I too had the desire to take refuge. When a person does this formally and ceremonially, she officially becomes a Buddhist. I was ready. In December, 2011, I joined Lama Dorjee at the KTC where he teaches *Dharma*, a Sanskrit word with roots in Hindu, Jain, and Buddhist philosophies that refers to the *sacred practice of ethical conduct and righteousness.*

We met each week for Lama Dorjee's teachings and group meditation. Some weekends, I joined other Sangha (community) members for additional sessions. A teaching on the *Heart Sutra* truly deepened my experience of my true self. This Sutra points directly to the nature of emptiness as the essence of all experience.

> "The cultivation of a twofold awareness where emptiness is a description of the background from which everything finds its meaning: It is reality as experienced by the enlightened

being. The opposite side of the same coin is the dissolution of the doer in life and consequently, the foundation of all cravings."[51]

When I embodied this awareness, Lama Dorjee gave me the Tibetan Buddhist name 'Karma Chen Chup Tharchen' which translates to 'Perfection of Bodhichitta Buddha Activity.'

I attended many of Lama Dorjee's teachings through the years and took pilgrimages with him to India, Nepal, Thailand, and Bhutan. In the winter of 2015, he asked me if I wanted to go with him and a group to Mount Kailash the next summer. I said "yes" without hesitation. Hindus and Buddhists as well as followers of Jain and Bon (a pre-Buddhist Tibetan religion) had been making the trip to Kailash for thousands of years. Walking in the footsteps of saints, sages, and other seekers who have bathed in the sacred gems that constitute the mountain's rock would be an opportunity of a lifetime. I could hardly imagine joining Lama Dorjee Rinpoche on the slopes of Mount Kailash, Tibet. And yet, it was to be.

Pilgrimage to Mount Kailash: A Place of Peace and Power

The seeds of this book were planted in meditation and revealed with the Desert Shaman and the insights I gained from my time with him. Yet the path forward remained unclear. All I knew was that the next stop on my journey of liberation would be in one of the most isolated sacred sites in the world, Mount Kailash in western Tibet. Oddly, although this trip turned out to be crucial for the continued chronicling of my healing journey, I planned it long before my experiences with the shaman and his decree that I write this book.

The week before I departed for Kailash, I had a vision during a craniosacral treatment. Craniosacral therapy uses gentle touch to manipulate the joints of the cranium. The practitioner encourages slight movement of the cranial sutures in rhythm with the breath. This manipulation assists the flow of cerebrospinal fluid around the brain and spinal cord and encourages deep relaxation as well as energy flow. As I drifted toward a sleepy state, I remained aware of my breath. Suddenly an image popped into my consciousness. I saw myself lying in a thin wooden casket that had no top. I was dressed all in white, and passersby tossed white flowers over my body. The vision dissipated after a few seconds. I didn't think this was a premonition of my impending death rather the signification of an end to something and, therefore, a new beginning. I imagined it had something to do with my upcoming pilgrimage to sacred land and left it at that.

Getting to remote western Tibet would be a feat in itself. The first leg would be to Beijing, China to spend the night. The next morning, we'd board a five-hour flight to Lhasa, the administrative capital of the Tibet Autonomous Region. We'd stay in this eastern part of the region (at 12,500 feet) for five days to acclimate to the elevation. Those of us from Texas were accustomed to living at a mere 500 feet above sea level. We'd tour monasteries and sacred sites, do some last-minute shopping. I'd take my backpack, compass and basic items from home and purchase hiking poles, glove liners and the like closer to our destination. Finally, we'd fly to Ali in western Tibet and travel hours by bus to Darchen, a small village at the base of Mount Kailash. We'd spend a day and a half at an altitude of 15,500 feet before proceeding to our three-day hike around the sacred mountain. In hindsight, my roomie and I needed more time to acclimate.

We knew going in, that the rugged 32-mile pathway around Mount Kailash is rife with harsh conditions, including uneven terrain, high altitude, steep inclines, and hostile weather. It takes at least 15 hours for a person in strong physical condition to get to Dolmala Pass, an elevation of nearly 18,600 feet. For a person in good health, it takes about three days to trek around the mountain. Some devotees, including Lama Dorjee, can do it in much less time. He was born in Tibet and was used to the terrain and elevation. For newbies, three days would be challenging enough.

The day finally arrived for us 21 adventurers and seekers to join Lama Dorjee and two tour guides for the trek around Kailash. We started hiking from the front door of our location in Darchin, at the base of the mountain. At 15,500 feet, it was fairly level terrain that slowly elevated. We started as a large group that eventually split into several small clusters as the thin air left some of us lagging behind.

My 70-year-old trail mate (and roommate for the duration of the trip) could barely get enough oxygen. I kept her in my sights as I walked ahead toward the top of hills to challenge myself against the arduous conditions, circling back often to see if she needed help or encouragement. After a few hours, one of the guides who'd been taking up the rear sidled up next to us.

Noticing that I walked faster than my companion, he suggested that I go on ahead. "I'll be back here with her," he whispered in a reassuring tone.

I tried to catch up with the rest of our group. It was to no avail. I was alone, trudging around an unknown mountain. I found myself in a quiet panic. 'Not finding my way home' has been a fear of mine for as long as I can remember. My muscles constricted. My breath got short and thin. I had to stop frequently to get my bearings and catch my breath. I did have an oxygen tank in my backpack. I didn't know until later that it was not just for emergencies and that the young guys with Lama Dorjee were using theirs often. At least the trails were visible at this point. Sleet, rain, and snow accompanied us for most of the rest of the first day.

I found our group at a rest point after about an hour. When my roommate entered my line of vision, my cold cheeks gave way to a beaming smile of relief. The front runners took off like a shot as I relaxed and prepared for the next leg. My roommate was still with a guide, so I was content to go on ahead. After another hour, I finally arrived at the lunch tent where we devoured food packed in from Darchen. I don't usually eat gluten-filled sandwiches, crackers, or cookies at home. Out on the trail, these foods provided great fuel. Unfortunately, my body wasn't used to that kind of eating, so it weakened as the trek progressed.

We made sure that the entire group got to the rest point and had lunch before we started back on the trail. The front runners separated quickly. After about 30 minutes, I got my stride back too, felt strong, and moved ahead of the pack at one point before stopping to rest. Then it started to rain. Then sleet, then snow. My water repellent jacket was warm, but it was no match for the icy gusts wafting across my back and face. I did not want to be separated from the group under these conditions. Instead of taking time to excavate my raincoat from my pack, I zipped up my vest and carried on. Shivering in the wet snow, I caught up to my fellow travelers.

Several hours passed when we came to a juncture. We could turn left over a bridge, go straight ahead, or veer to the right. We didn't know which way to go, and neither of our guides were around. I assumed that one of them was back with my roomie and the other was in the lead. We had to decide for ourselves which way to go. There were ten of us who crossed that bridge together with Lama Dorjee who was unfamiliar with that juncture.

After about a mile, a pale-yellow structure in the distance came into view on the other side of the river. According to the map, this building was to be our shelter for the night. It was clear that we'd made the wrong choice back at the crossroads and would have to retrace our steps. We turned around and plodded back to the bridge. By the time that we got there I was soaked to my bones, my chattering teeth serving as a relentless reminder of a series of unskillful decisions. And where were the guides?

As soon as we crossed the river I stopped to find my raincoat and neck warmer. The added layers offered instant reprieve. When I looked up, everyone was gone. It was that same 'Y' in the path that gave us trouble before, and I didn't know which way the group went. How could they leave me? I realized that their aim was to get Lama Dorjee to the shelter. I still felt left behind. At least my odds for making the right decisions about which trail to take improved since I only had two options this time, straight ahead or to the right. It was getting dark and fear sneaked up on me. Rather than forging down the wrong path I decided to stay put for a few minutes and wait for guidance, Supreme or otherwise.

Fortunately, several hikers came along. Unfortunately, they didn't speak English and I didn't speak their languages either. I didn't want to be alone in foul weather on a trail I didn't know, so I shadowed them up a steep incline to 'somewhere.' Exhausted, I kept moving with the hope that I would see or find someone from my group. After about thirty minutes, I recognized three people. We collected ourselves and discussed our options. We concluded that we'd have to walk down the mountain, about 90 degrees from the trail we were on, to get to the shelter. It was pitch black. With flashlights, we stumbled down the muddy slope to our safe haven for the night.

The shelter was modest at best. It had no lights or heat. The toilets were behind any boulder out back and there was no running water. Having a roof over our heads, warm blankets, and a flashlight was more than sufficient after the day we'd had. When I got to my room, I put on dry clothes and sat on my twin bed with such a sense of relief that my heart spilled with gratitude. I closed my eyes, soaking in the warmth and solitude.

My blissful state didn't last long. My roommate was missing. In fact, after taking a headcount we learned that three people were unaccounted for. One of our group members ran back down the trail, flashlight in hand, to look for the missing. He found my roomie at the dreaded Y intersection, freezing and delirious, saying over and over, "I'm going to die out here!" He tried to comfort her as he walked her back toward the shelter. The other two missing members spotted them and followed behind.

My roomie came into our room yelling, "I'm going to die! If I don't die tonight I'll probably die tomorrow because I can't do this anymore." I helped her pull off her wet clothes and wrapped her in blankets. Damp clothes and gloves were strewn about the room, so I hung hers up on random nails and the ends of curtain rods. The four of us staying in that room all tried to stay calm. Hypothermia was not what we anticipated to be on the menu that night, and we really hoped to avoid it. She finally settled down and warmed up. I meticulously peeled each page of her drenched passport apart and left it, fanned open, on the nightstand to dry.

Later we found out that the guide left her on the trail to find her own way. He hurried ahead because he was told to prepare food for the evening meal. Several of us were furious with the tour company for sending only two guides for 21 people. There was no turning back. We hiked eleven hours that first day out in the elements. It should have taken six.

On Day 2 on Mount Kailash, we woke before sunup. Fueled with boiled eggs, porridge, and tea we set out for the day's schlep toward Dolmala Pass. At 18,600 feet, this would be the highest elevation of the hike. By dawn, the rain had stopped. The skies were dark and cloudy as we started up another muddy trail. The clouds brightened and the air warmed. Some of the trails were sopping wet from the rain, sleet and snow that pummeled the mountain the day before.

After climbing for hours over rocks and boulders, I had no strength to carry my pack and keep my balance. The air was thin, and I wasn't the only person wondering how we'd all get to the Pass intact. I found a Sherpa for hire to carry my pack. Hikers at Kailash frequently rely on members of an ethnic group called Sherpas who live on the borders of Nepal and Tibet to help them deal with the most difficult terrain. Having lived at these high altitudes for generations, they are highly skilled mountaineers and acclimated to the thin air. Others in our group, including my roommate, managed the final two days on horseback.

On the way to Dolmala Pass, I noticed a translucent-like, grey boulder on the right-hand side of the path. Transfixed, I stepped off the trail to take a closer look. *It was as though I recognized it.* I knew it was the stone marker my Reiki teacher told me about. During one of our sessions before my trip to Tibet, she told me about a stone throne on Mount Kailash for meditating on 11th chakra healing. In the chakra system, the 11th chakra 'governs your ability to transcend space and time.'

As I walked around the stone marker, I saw the throne with its V-shaped back and seat nestled between the two boulders making up its sides. I gathered myself and sat down on the cold, hard surface to meditate on the 11th chakra as my reiki teacher and the Desert Shaman suggested. I closed my eyes and took a breath. The color purple emerged in my inner field of vision, glowing and moving at will. I exhaled slowly. Energy moved downward, extending beyond my body in the direction of the earth's center. On my next breath, I visualized and felt the energy simultaneously move upward, past the crown of my head toward an infinite sky. There was no endpoint to this line of energy. I felt expansiveness in all directions, and did not particularly notice my dense body.

The 11th chakra (energy center) is said to be about 15 feet above one's head; the energy itself, unbounded. Healing this chakra helps people to deal with experiences beyond the physical, opening the individual to multiple dimensions and planes of existence. 'Mind blowing' is the best way I can think of to describe it. Incidentally, nirvana actually means the *blown-out state*.[52]

I was in this meditative space about ten minutes, until two of my hiking companions walked up to take a picture of me. Somewhat startled, I got my bearings and joined them back on the trail. They sent me the photos (below) after we all returned home. Etchings on the left-hand stone resembled Mayan petroglyphs yet the Mayans were on another continent. My mind wandered momentarily as I wondered whether another migration was left out of the history books. The inscriptions did not look Tibetan, Chinese or Egyptian. I pondered their meaning with the understanding that I would never know for sure. I marveled once again at the miracle of finding the throne at all.

Karen Meditating on the throne; Mount Kailash, Tibet. See message inscribed on stone"

We arrived at Dolmala pass, also known as The Pass of the Noble Mother Tara, after about a 4-hour hike. Andrea Miller in the book *Buddha's Daughters* explains that the Noble Mother Tara vanished beneath a large stone after helping a monk get to the top of the Pass. The stone was adorned and carved with mantras to commemorate her disappearance.[53]

On this still and peaceful day, we witnessed the sacred Dolmala Stone and joined our voices in song to honor Mother Tara's selfless generosity and to pray for healing and blessings to all beings. I placed a prayer flag that I'd carried with me on the trip. It had been absorbing mantras and prayers on my altar for months that could now be released into the air as the flag flaps in the breeze. I quieted my mind and immersed myself in the vibrant energy of this hallowed place. This is what enlightened beings have felt and left for others on this Mountain for thousands of years.

The lead group left Domala Pass shortly after the last of us arrived, me being one of them. I took my time and eventually started to amble back down the path toward the Monastery, more than four hours away where we would spend the night. My toes jammed into the front of my boots as I moved downhill. I stopped to rest, readjust my socks, and tighten my boots. What a privilege to have such gear!

It took me about an hour and a half to catch up with the rest of the group. By then my toes were screaming. I asked one of the guides if there was a horse available for the rest of the trek down to the Monastery. They rustled one up, and I joined my roomie on horseback after having some butter tea and lunch. When we arrived, we were all whipped yet elated to have a place to prop our feet and recover. Four of us shared a comfortable, ornamented room. It was a far cry from our accommodations on the first leg, and we enjoyed every moment of it.

The next day we hiked down to the base of the mountain into Darchen. I moved quickly most of the time. The portable spray oxygen tank made a world of difference in my stamina. I reached the north side of the base camp Darchen and sat on a bench soaking up the beauty of the mountains. Thirty minutes later I was happy to see my roomie and several others coming down the trail. The end was near.

We offloaded our backpacks. Most of my cohort ventured by bus to the southern foot of Mount Kailash to visit the world's highest freshwater lake, Lake Manasarovar with its vibrant blue shores and emerald center. Already full with experiences yet too vast for me to understand or describe, I stayed behind to take a long bath and take care of a cough I developed on the trek. I was exhausted and knew I could not make another excursion. I chose to rest and nurture myself.

The next day we had breakfast and loaded onto the bus for our 4-hour ride to the Ali airport where we would fly to Lhasa, Tibet. We met Lama Dorjee's relatives over the next two days before flying to Beijing, China. I could see Lama Dorjee with his Tibetan relatives brimming with joy and humor after so many years apart.

Karen Ibarguen at the base of Mount Kailash

While I was sightseeing in Beijing my cough worsened, even though I wore a mask outside. I was coughing up bright red blood by the time I arrived home. It freaked me out as I had always considered myself to be a strong, healthy woman. Not after this trip. I was in bed for three days asking myself how I was going to function in this condition, let alone evaluate and treat patients. My reality was shaken, life more confusing. I knew I was in the midst of a major transformation and needed to ride it out.

It took several months after Kailash for me to regain my strength. The last week of December (2016), five months after my return, I became very ill with a stomach virus and upper respiratory infection. I had a full schedule of patients that day until about 5:00 PM. Chills quickly turned to shivers and shakes, until the whole of my body began to quake. I called my last patient to cancel their appointment, locked up my office and headed home. The one-block walk that typically felt like an easy stroll was a marathon. When I finally arrived at home, I filled a glass with water and dragged myself into bed, pulling the blankets over my head to quell the building pressure. It didn't work. I put an ice pack at the base of my skull to get some relief, and fell asleep.

When I awoke, I felt weak and had no appetite. I drank a small glass of ginger, lemon and honey water before falling back to sleep. All the while focusing my attention on my heart and breath, I remained calm and centered. Yet I knew I was sick and getting sicker. I called my dear friend Eva to see if she could come over. She had family in town and was already nursing someone at home after surgery. I thought I could make it on my own until she could come by the day after the New year.

My natural remedy worked for one day, and then stopped working. I kept getting weaker and weaker. Pupils dilated and skin as white as a sheet, I thought to myself: "I do not want to leave this life. But if it is meant to be, I am at peace." I had a deep sense of knowing that although my body may cease to exist, my eternal Self will never die. Just as Yogananda recounted the deathless essence of the Bible as Christ's eternal words, I too, an embodied soul would live beyond the passing of heaven and earth.[54]

Suddenly, I had a flashback. The day before the onset of the sickness, I had a craniosacral treatment. And just as I did before I went to Kailash, I saw a vision. In that vision, my motionless body lay in a primitive wooden casket, dressed in white with white flowers around my head. This was the same vision that I had five months earlier, before leaving for Mount Kailash. Was this a premonition of a life-threatening illness and my possible demise?

Eva knocked at my door. As she came in, her eyes widened and jaw dropped. I could tell that she was trying not to reveal how shocked she was to see me in this startling condition. As I passed by the mirror by the door I heard myself say, "Oh goodness, I do look pretty bad." Sunken, dilated eyes, and gray gaunt skin reflected back at me.

"Does your family know how sick you are?" she asked. "Yes. I called my sister to get the word out to the rest of the family that I was very ill."

We chatted for a moment before I had to lie down again. I poured onto my mattress on the floor. Eva sat next to me and held her hands just above my body. I could feel a buzz of energy. She lightly touched my belly, then softly pulled the tissue toward her and then away to the opposite side. As she kneaded my flesh back and forth in gentle motion, she thanked my body for protecting me and holding those unconscious memories that seeded my journey toward liberation. I started to cry.

I listened to Eva's words and brought her statement of gratitude into my heart. As I breathed, I could feel the tight, gnawing energy flow out of my body towards the sky. My body calmed. Eva sat at my feet and did a little more energy work before pulling the covers up to my neck and slipping out the door. I bathed in my new-found body and quickly fell asleep.

The next day I felt alert and alive again. Still weak, the task at hand was to rebuild my body. I strolled that single block to my office and picked up a homeopathic remedy. It kicked in right away. This was the start of a new chapter.

My outlook on life is different now that I know I am not in complete control of it. People come and go in our lives for a reason. Johnny, my beautiful friend Eva, Mooji, Kevin Snow, Lama Dorjee and the others who either crossed my path or walked with me on it for a while. My quest has been to look inward to discover the vastness of my existence at all times as I move through life. There is a knowing that I am *That*. Yet, this knowing still only hints at the underlying "I" of all existence. As the *Yoga Sutras* teach, we can come to realize that true happiness does not exist outside of us, as something to be attained. There is an ever present, abiding oneness that is eternally within each and every one of us. We are capable of being receptive to the internal connection where "The Seer abides in Itself, resting in its own True Nature, which is called Self-realization."[55] We are worthy of love.

Chapter 6

OPENING TO YOUR OWN JOURNEY

Gloomy clouds burn away so that we can see the light in us that was already there, all along.

Neil Spencer, Artist and Author exploring
Yoga, Meditation, and the Human Brain [56]

A human being's essential nature has no agenda with the mind, body, or world. It is pure awareness, like an empty space within which all things manifest. This allowing cultivates love, tolerance, and resilience. Fundamentally, our main purpose is to bring ourselves to a place of openness and love of ourselves and others. Knowing *That* comes from a process of spiritual transformation not wholly unlike the transmutation of lead into gold.

Alchemical Transformation

> Alchemy is actually fixated on spiritual development - with the end goal being a state of completion, awareness and harmony.
>
> *--Labyrinthos Academy, 2017*

The medieval forerunner of chemistry known as alchemy spanned continents and philosophical traditions for millennia. Although focused on the transmutation of matter, many alchemists emphasized the metaphysical and spiritual aspects. Just as base metals can be transmuted into gold,[57] the human spirit can metamorphose in an evolution to enlightenment.

The Labyrinthos Academy describes the alchemical process of transformation in terms of being broken, remade, tested and reborn again - a perfect summation of my life-long quest to heal hidden wounds and seek liberation. They explain that the chemical transfiguration of a substance from calcination to coagulation mirrors the transformation of the human being from the breakdown of ego to the perception of life on all levels of consciousness. It's a seven-stage process: (1) calcination, (2) dissolution, (3) separation, (4) conjunction, (5) fermentation, (6) distillation, and (7) coagulation.[58]

Figure 4: Seven Stages of Alchemical Transformation

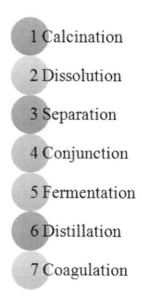

1 Calcination

2 Dissolution

3 Separation

4 Conjunction

5 Fermentation

6 Distillation

7 Coagulation

The stages of transformation do not necessarily flow in the neat, linear order that enables them to be conceptualized and accessible to people. There is an ebb to that flow, and sometimes seekers will move back and forth between or among stages for periods of time until reaching a new level of awareness. That said, I describe each of the alchemical stages and how I see my own journey captured within them.

In alchemy, for example, *calcination* refers to the burning of matter until it turns to ash. On one's spiritual journey this means breaking attachments to all things that feed the psychologically constructed sense of self known as the ego. Letting go of everything that defines personal identity – from social and economic status, to nationality, race, or religion, to emotions, opinions and personal stories of triumph, loss, abandonment, suffering, trauma, and so on—allows us to realize that the ego is not who we really are. Burning the ego to ash sparks a self-inquiry that goes beyond what the mind alone can understand or rationalize. It is the first step in asking ourselves who we really are.

I've had quite a few experiences that went beyond what

my mind alone could rationalize, some conspicuous enough to disrupt my thinking mind to the degree that I had to shed the illusion that I understand myself or my world at all. Many people have experienced the inexplicable only to brush it off as insignificant, imaginary, or coincidental. A vision. A voice. A feeling of having been somewhere before. A moment of clarity in which suddenly you know something to be true, or not true. In these moments, the mind expands beyond its usual capacity. Something out of the ordinary breaks through. The ego, set aside for the time being, embeds the seed of self-inquiry within one's consciousness. A journey begins.

How else might I explain listening to a mantra and hearing a voice inside myself saying "You must give up who you think you are." Seeing myself in a forest clearing wearing a long red cloak and dancing around an enormous bonfire as I sensed American Indian form and rhythm. A transformative dance of initiation to burn up my individual self and unite with the collective.

The process of chemical *dissolution* dissolves the ash in water. Likewise, human beings plunge into the unconscious to uncover parts of ourselves that were hidden beneath the ego and its incessant demarcations and storylines. Be they conditioned beliefs, reactive patterns, or memories too disturbing to bring into the conscious mind, this stage invites us to release the constructs that limit our perceptions of who we are.

As I started my process of self-inquiry and realized the limits of ego, I sought to let them go as much as I humanly could. I found healers and therapeutic modalities along the way that opened new ways of feeling and consciously moving the energy in and around my body. As I became aware of subtle energy flows and sensations, the hidden wound from my childhood trauma surfaced to the point that I could feel it, remember it, and begin a process of healing and self-discovery. I began to discern how this and other traumas shaped my self-concept and my understandings of my life, relationships, circumstances, and purpose.

In *separation*, the alchemist filters out and separates the products of dissolution. Similarly, after discovering the beliefs, emotions, memories, narratives, and habits previously hidden deep within the unconscious, the spiritual seeker can sift through them to recognize which ones diminish who we are, and which ones help us to grow.

As I started to become aware that all experiences create imprints on the mind, I realized that my habits, beliefs, and perceptions of myself and others were not actually real: They were impressions. Some produced positive actions in my life, such as *surviving* sexual assault and working hard to succeed against the odds; others generated negative behaviors like chemical addictions to distract myself and staying away from close relationships to create a semblance of safety. It is not surprising that when I started learning about self-inquiry and began to practice it faithfully, I found a soul sister to share it with and a guru to impart lessons I needed to learn. That silent retreat in Portugal with Mooji introduced me to the philosophy of Advaita and the truth of nondual consciousness, or oneness of Being. From that point on, I was committed to cleansing and nourishing myself so that I could relinquish that which no longer serves and move toward self-transformation.

Conjunction is the process of combining selected elements after separation. This is the point of reintegration, where the conscious and unconscious interface. Once aware of the hidden constructs that fed the ego, we are no longer tethered to their demands. These shadow aspects of the self, now in the light of consciousness, no longer have the same influence. We can put them in their place and use them to grow.

After experiencing the ocean of consciousness, my ego no longer held the same sway. It was there, of course. It just didn't rule with the omnipotence it once had. Living at an ashram with Mooji and a community of seekers reinforced this shift in consciousness and helped me to unpeel who I thought I was. Intentionally loosening the tight grip that I had on Dr. Karen—the ego-centric human being ruled by personality, identity, belief, and past experiences—opened a pathway for me to become *Sanoja*, my eternal Self. Not just when I meditated but throughout my daily routine of work, food, lifestyle, relationships, and the transient stuff of life that have no bearing on the infinite.

The chemical process of *fermentation* continues to break down the substance by introducing living organisms like bacteria. Alchemically, this is a test of the reintegrated self. As life unfolds, we will face difficulties that test our new sense of self. In doing so, we have opportunities to fortify ourselves.

The breakdown and replacement of habitual patterns do not occur automatically. There are bouts of setbacks and ameliorations, deterioration and recovery that may recur over multiple periods of time before the new self takes hold. Crucial episodes on my journey tested me physically, mentally, emotionally and spiritually. That 10-week stint in Portugal with Mooji pulled me in so many directions that I was overwhelmed until the silent retreat allowed me to feel, and be aware of, my eternal Self. Yet, this was nothing compared to putting my life on the line on Mount Kailash in Tibet. The wear and tear on my body coupled with emotional turmoil revealed my deepest and most lasting internal search.

In *distillation*, the substance is purified by boiling and condensing the solution that results from fermentation. To prepare for the final stage of spiritual transformation, the spirit must be freed from the destructive aspects of the ego that encourage the mind to create unnecessary boundaries between the individual and the collective. The Labyrinthos Academy explains that, "Here we are planting the seed for the unborn, transpersonal self...To help it grow, one has to nourish it - which can be done with various forms of contemplation, spiritual ritual or meditation."

The distillation process laid bare the essence of my true Self. In fact, when I returned from Mount Kailash, I could not identify with myself as Dr. Karen at all. After embracing a deeper sense of Self, I had no idea how to be the self with the small 's.' I did not know how to be functional in the world without losing, once again, that self-expansion. In this stage of transformation, my meditation and spiritual work helped me to integrate the two selves. I could be, as they say, a *spiritual being having a human experience.* With a pure spirit, I could be functional in the world and still be aware of my true self.

Whereas *coagulation* crystalizes the substance into a solid state, the human spirit has become self-aware in a union of dualities. The inner and outer world are simply reflections of each other.

Although it may be tempting to view the stages of spiritual transformation as completely linear, movement through and across stages at different times is more common as human beings realize, and then forget, who they really are. When coagulation is palpable, however, human beings can sense and know that there is no difference, truly, between matter and spirit. Those moments of illumination profoundly impact a person's life. When I thought I was on my deathbed on the last day of 2016, I knew without any doubt that I was the same eternal Self with or without a body. My eternal being is where all experience takes place and out of which all experience is made. Spirit and matter, all one Consciousness.

Throughout my own process of alchemical transformation, I've come to know my essential nature and purpose not from my thinking mind but from the subtler aspects of my Self. Awareness always starts the same way: Taking time to sit, breathe, and notice the present moment.

Mindfulness Practices to Help You Along Your Path

Taking time out of one's day to sit with one's breath sounds simple. It is, and it isn't. Breathing techniques are simple in that they involve something we already know how to do, and do automatically; breathe in and out. They're challenging because life can get so hectic that when we have a few moments to sit quietly, the mind often continues to race. Stress, illness, or injury can also constrict the breath, making it shallow and seemingly less soothing.

Even so, mindful breathing practices help us to get calm, become more self-aware, and heal from the traumas - big and small - that we experience throughout our lives. I've never regretted taking a time out to sit and breathe. Doing so places the intention of opening to my essential nature to live my life's purpose front and center, where the deepest healing and restoration can occur. Mindful breathing calms the nervous system, sharpens focus, and opens a doorway to knowing one's higher self.

I invite you to try some mindfulness practices of your own. I've shared simple instructions about how to create a short, daily breathing practice. If you like, you can expand your practice to include a mindful body scan. These exercises give you a set of tools to learn how to breathe deeply and cultivate your awareness of the present moment while acknowledging and accepting any feelings, thoughts, or sensations that arise.

First, take a moment to acknowledge that you want to heal. Say out loud, "I am ready to heal" or "Thank you for this healing." These statements create a resonance of attraction - the inspirations, challenges, resources, allowance, and resolve that will be part of your healing journey. You already have what you need. You are on the path. With this burning desire to heal, Grace makes it happen. Indeed, true healing occurs in no other way.

Sit with Your Breath

Everything is a manifestation of Spirit. It is ever-present in mundane activities if we are aware of it.

1. **Take 2 minutes out of your day.** This might be upon waking in the morning before you're off and running, at lunch when you have a few minutes to yourself, when you get home from work, or just before going to sleep.

2. **Find a quiet spot.** It doesn't matter where you sit. Find a place that soothes you and where you won't be interrupted. In nature, on a park bench, looking out a window where you see trees blowing in the wind, or in a quiet corner of your office or bedroom. Be creative, and make this a place of your own. Some enjoy creating an altar of meaningful objects such as a Bible, a picture of loved one, elements of nature such as crystals, rock formations, pine cones, or shells you picked up during your favorite vacation.

3. **Sit comfortably.** This can be in a chair, on a cushion, against a wall or in a meditation posture. Sit in a relaxed way with your back straight. Some people prefer sitting on the floor. Just keep your spine long and your body comfortable.

4. **Relax**. Close your eyes. Unclench your jaw. Soften your face. Let your muscles get a little slack, using just enough energy to hold yourself in your seat.

5. **Breathe.** As you breathe in slowly through your nose, feel your breath move through your nostrils. As you breathe out, feel the warmth of your breath as it passes back through the nostrils. If you prefer, breath in through your nose and out your mouth. Maybe count your breaths as you go. Breathing in, one. Breathing out, two. All the way to ten. If you lose track, start over.

6. **Repeat this breathing practice for a few minutes.** It is normal for the mind to stay active throughout this process. Let the mind's thoughts come and go as you gently bring your focus back to your breath each time. Refocusing the mind from thought to breath is not about pushing thoughts away or pretending they shouldn't exist. It's a matter of repetitively refocusing to the breath which allows us to be present. Human beings love making stories out of things. There's no need for that. This is a moment to sit with the breath, not the mind. Stay neutral to whatever comes up.

Note: You can record the directions in steps 4 and 5 and play them back to guide you through your practice. It's a great way to get started.

The Mindful Body Scan

Sitting quietly and paying attention to the breath is a great way to calm down and focus one's attention. It can also be a bridge to other mindfulness practices such as the mindful body scan. Here's how to do it.

1. **Commit to 5 minutes each day.** Same time, same place (if possible), and same opening breathing exercise.

2. **Begin with your breathing practice.** Use the same instructions as above. If you are not overly inclined to fall asleep, try this one lying on your back. If you find yourself falling asleep, return to a comfortable seated position.

3. **Do a full scan of your body while continuing to breathe slowly.** Bring your attention to your toes. Gently wiggling your toes can help. Notice what you feel. Tingling, warmth, cold, heaviness? Next, shift your focus to your feet, then to your lower legs, thighs, hips and torso. **Pause in between each area and notice any sensations you feel as you contract and relax that part of your body.** Spontaneous movements might occur, such as a twitch or sudden jumping of one of your limbs. Let it happen and move along, focusing your attention systematically upward to each part of your body.

Notice that when you breathe, your torso expands in **all** directions, laterally as well as front and back. When you focus on your fingers, wiggle them if you like. Sense your hands, arms, and shoulders. Soften your neck. Feel your cheeks, your forehead and your scalp. Just as you might have wiggled your fingers and toes, you might squint your face to bring about a fuller sensation.

After you reach the top of your head, travel your attention all the way back down to where you started, feeling each area of your body along the way after the area relaxes.

Take as much time as you need. The mindful body scan reconnects your attention to *feeling the body* instead of thinking and doing.

An Awareness Exercise

In addition to breathing practices, one can cultivate awareness through *singular focus*, by taking time out to bring attention to a person, place, or thing. The 'object' of this practice can be anything or anyone. A pet sleeping on a blanket, a friend practicing guitar, a tree branch moving outside the window, a lamp on the side table, the eyes of our beloved. The task is to observe the object without judging it or labeling it. Simply observe your object of regard as part of your present existence, as one with your surroundings.

1. **Commit to 5 minutes on any given day.** Pick a location, indoors or outdoors.

2. **Sit in a comfortable position. Focus your gaze on any one thing.** (It is easy to start by gazing on an object across the room). Look upon the object without judging or evaluating it, thereby allowing the mind to rest and the body to soften and relax. As you look upon the

object, notice if you could be five or ten percent more comfortable. Is there tension behind your eyes that could soften? Could you relax your neck and shoulders a bit more, or ease tightness in your chest? Soften your body as you look upon your object. Linger there for a few moments. Feel this space and presence.

3. **Become subtly aware of your surroundings as you gaze upon an object.** Feel the awareness outside your body. Linger there and feel your presence. Gaze upon another object in the room and include it in the tableau of your experience. Know that there are things behind, above and below you; existence in all directions, not just what you can see. Take a few moments. You may notice a sense of expansion.

4. **Close your eyes. Can you still feel the presence of your object, the space and all that surrounds you whether you see it or not?** As you practice this awareness exercise, you may come to know that awareness has no boundaries, edges or endpoint. In this way, awareness goes beyond only noticing the senses of the body or the thoughts of the mind. Awareness is where this *being* experiences all of life. Its essence could be considered one's true Self. Inquire on this. 'What' is noticing, or is aware of, your experience?

Connecting to Your Heart Space

Awareness and mindfulness practices help to release the tensions and stressors accumulated throughout the day. Quieting the mind allows the body to relax as you become aware of subtle movements or energies that you don't ordinarily notice. Such awareness helps the practitioner to get in touch with the inner, eternal Self. Opening the heart space with meditative breathing is another way to do this.

1. **Commit to 10 minutes each day.** Same time, same place (if possible).

2. **Begin with your breathing practice** or listen to the instructions in your own voice as recorded on your phone or other device.

3. **Connect to your heart space.** Once you've calmed your body and relaxed your mind, lightly place your hand on your chest. Notice that there is a soft space beneath the palm of your hand that does not touch the body, the heart of your palm.

Focus your attention to that 'heart space' while breathing in a slow, comfortable rhythm. Feel for warmth under your palm as you breathe. You may notice a pulsation, vibration, or feeling of subtle movement under or around your hand. Stay with this sensation for a few moments.

4. **Notice whether your mind is more quiet and peaceful.** As you practice connecting with your 'heart space' daily,

it is possible that you will be able to sense it without placing your palm at your chest at all. As you become more aware of the dynamic movement of energy in and around your body, you may notice how it expands or contracts along with your thoughts and feelings.

5. **Notice how your practice changes each day.** It can be beneficial to keep a few notes of what happened as you connected to your heart space. Write as much or as little as you like. Reread your notes occasionally to observe how your awareness shifts.

Asking "What Does Life Want?"

Awareness resides as a human being's true body and essential nature. Its vibrant presence lacks nothing. It needs no money, no lover, no job, no need to be accepted by anyone. Complete in itself, awareness is where intuition (deep knowing) resides. By meditating on the heart space to connect with the eternal Self, we can ask questions like "What does life want?" or "What does God want?" In moments of stillness the subtle body responds to the question asked, as contraction or expansion. This practice cultivates profound connection to that inner intuitive self.

1. **Commit to 15 minutes each day.**
2. **Begin with your breathing practice.**
3. **Connect to your heart space.** With your attention on the heart space, breathe in and out slowly for several minutes. Notice any sensations of warmth or a subtle movement in the heart space, especially near the end of an exhalation.

4. **Look for inner wisdom.** When you feel calm and centered, ask yourself: "What does life want?" Linger and notice as you ask the question whether you feel a sense of expansion or a contraction in the body or heart space.

A sense of expansion suggests an openness, or an allowing of whatever life brings. Feelings of contraction suggest a resistance. There is no need to judge your feeling. Just notice. You may repeat the question or ask yourself another question that you have been pondering. Feel for an allowing or a resistance as you remain in your meditative state.

5. **Notice how your practice changes each day**. As with the heart space meditation, you may want to keep track of your experiences and insights as you hone your intuition.

Processing the Practice and Taking It with You

Have you noticed that all through your life experience has always been 'here,' never there? Wherever you are, it's 'here.' Just like every moment in time you have experienced has been 'now.' 'Now' is not limited to any particular moment in time, just like 'here' is not limited to any particular place in space. The 'here' and 'now' are infinite eternal Consciousness.

'That' is where experience takes place and what experience is made of.

> In order for eternity to appear as time and infinity
> to appear as space; Infinite Consciousness must
> forget the knowing of its own being, and must
> limit itself which it does by appearing in and as
> the body. That is why we see the world from the
> perspective of the body.
>
> *Rupert Spira, author of* Consciousness
> is Our True Body [59]

For any of these mindfulness practices, keeping a journal about one's experiences can be fruitful, and it doesn't take much time. Using a pen and paper instead of a keyboard unites the mind and body in profound ways.

Take a few moments at the end of your practice to write down anything that comes to mind. Include words, colors or images that entered your thought space during your practice; ideas that came to you; memories that streamed through your mind; sensations you experienced from an itch to a taste to buzzing in your ear. It doesn't matter if the words make sense to you or come out in complete sentences. Follow your heart and let the words and images flow freely. If you remember something later on, write it down as soon as you get the chance.

As with any therapeutic exercise, spontaneously arising emotions are a normal and healthy part of healing. Here too, journaling may be especially helpful when emotional challenges surface as exploring them can help to uncover their roots. That being said, identifying root causes is not necessary for healing to occur. Learning how to discharge emotional wounds from the body at their own pace is central to healing holistically.

To heal deep emotional wounds, we must tune in to the felt sense. To feel and allow feelings, sensations, and emotions to occur and hold them in steadiness with the breath until they naturally dissipate. Although such release might occur in a single setting, the emotional landscape changes along with the sensory experiences that accompany them. It often takes several sessions for unconscious emotions held within the body to be revealed.

Getting in touch with one's internal experiences as they occur in the present moment helps to unlock bound-up emotional energy and its imprints in the body.

If the emotion of sadness arises, for example, notice how it shows up in the body. Does it contract your chest? Quicken your heart rate? Come out as trembling tears? Sit like a boulder in the bottom of your gut? Rather than allowing the mind to create a story about the meaning of the emotion, notice what it feels like in your body. Allow it to grow if that's what needs to happen, all the while maintaining a focus on the breath. As you imagine moving the feeling into your heart space it will start to dissolve at its own pace, eventually disappearing altogether.

If anger arises follow the same protocol. Observe where and how it shows up in your body. You may get a chill or start to sweat, feel a pain or tingling, have a sense of emptiness. Felt sensations run the gamut. Just feel them as you notice your breath move in and out. Use your mind's eye to move the feeling into the heart space as you allow it exist and then to fade. Another way to feel the heart space would be to lightly touch the thumb and finger pads of your right hand together at your sternum while keeping your palm soft. Hold this position as you take a slow breath in and out. Continue to breathe in this way until you feel the emotion dissolve.

If a feeling such as anger is so strong that sitting with the breath is not possible, other actions may be used to calm the body first. Screaming into a pillow literally dissipates negative energy through the vibration and movement required to make the sound. Throwing a small plastic bottle to the floor and watching it bounce high into the air can free pent-up energy in the body, transmitting it to an object safely. It can be extremely cathartic!

After the body relaxes, take a comfortable seat. Follow your breath. Notice where the residue of the emotion still resides. Allow it to exist. Sit with it. Bring your attention to the space of your heart or breath. This process allows a strong emotion, once unconscious, to arise fully so that it may diminish safely and at its own pace.

As we get in touch with inner wisdom to release blocked energy in the body, we begin to develop greater awareness. In time, we realize that there is more to being than simply one's physicality, thoughts, senses, and emotions. In observing what comes up in meditation, noticing the breath, watching ourselves sit or act, or feeling a rush of sensation, we discover a deeper Self. This awareness comes not from the mind. By identifying ourselves as the *observer* or *seer* we experience a deeper, more subtle Self that is ever present.

Practicing mindfulness opens up possibilities to be in the

world without getting caught up in its many dramas. When we are no longer tethered to our unconscious stories, twitchy nervous systems, and buried emotional wounds, joy and sound decisions are more likely to occur.

This doesn't mean we have to give up our lives, move to a commune, or spend hours a day on a meditation cushion. Mindfulness can happen anywhere, in line at the grocery store or stopped at a traffic light. Just pause. Take a moment to breathe in a rhythm. You might even place your hand on your heart and sense the weight of your feet on the ground as you consciously breathe. Notice as the heartbeat slows down and the body relaxes. Be aware that you are breathing as long as your mind will allow it.

Every experience of presence and calm no matter how momentary, allows us to see our deeper self. The more you practice mindful moments throughout your day, the more you will feel connected to your essential nature. This, too, is a process of alchemical transformation. As you nurture your own spiritual development, you will come to know your essential nature and purpose, not from the thinking mind but from the subtler aspects of the eternal Self.

IMAGES AND FIGURES

Image #	Caption	Source	Page
Image 1	Moth	Photo by Warren Photographic	xvi
Image 2	Cathedral Rock; Sedona, Arizona	Photo by Scott McAllister, Art Collections.	23
Image 3	Bell Rock; Sedona, Arizona	Photo by Scott McAllister, Art Collections.	25
Image 4	Kogi Mamos; Colombia, South America	Released from Kogi trip coordinator.	29
Image 5	Petroglyphs: History of the Kogi Mamos	Released from Kogi trip coordinator.	30
Image 6	Eva Hunter; Colombia, South America	Photo from the author.	32
Image 7	Karen Ibarguen meditating at the Ocean; Colombia, South America	Photo from the author.	32
Image 8	Alchemical Tarot Deck	Released from Robert M. Place, See also: Place, Robert. (1995). *The Alchemical Tarot*. London: Harper Collins.	56
Image 9	Prayer Ties from Ceremony	Photo from the author.	77

Image 10	Medicine Wheel	Photo from the author.	78
Image 11	Karen meditating on the 'throne; Mount Kailash, Tibet	Photo from the author.	133
Image 12	Karen meditating on the throne. See message inscribed on stone.	Photo from the author.	133
Image 13	Karen Ibarguen at the base of Mount Kailash	Photo from the author.	135

Figure 1	Four Body Quadrants and their Primary Content	Figure created by Gayle Sulik, PhD	60
Figure 2	Elements of the Medicine Wheel	Table created by Gayle Sulik, PhD	79
Figure 3	Adverse Childhood Experiences (ACEs) Study Depicting Outcomes Later in Life	Adverse Childhood Experiences (ACEs) are strongly related to the development and prevalence of a wide range of health problems throughout a person's lifespan, including those associated with substance use disorders. This graphic is used courtesy of the Substance Abuse and Mental Health Services Administration (SAMHSA), U.S. Department of Health and Human Services (HHS). Use of this graphic does not constitute or imply endorsement by SAMHSA or HHS of content or opinions in this book.	112
Figure 4	Seven Stages of Alchemical Transformation	Figure created by Gayle Sulik, PhD	141

REFERENCES AND ENDNOTES

1   Chopra, Deepak. "Harness Your Mind's Power to Heal and Transform." The Chopra Center. Accessed July. 1, 2017. http://www.chopra.com/ articles/harness-your-mind's-power-to-heal-and-transform#sm.00014qv qe25ixe2quuo14useyd9lz

2   Zoll, Stuart J. (1994). *The Bridge Between Acupuncture and Modern Bio-Energetic Medicine*. Germany: Haug (Karl F.) Verlag GmbH & Co.

3   Felitti, V.J., Anda, R.F., Nordenberg, D., Williamson, D.F., Spitz, A., Edwards, V., Koss, M.P., Marks, J.S. (1998). "Relationship of Childhood and Household Dysfunction to Many of the Leading Causes of Death in Adults." *American Journal of Preventive Medicine*,14(4): 245-58.

4   Quote attributed to Damasio, Antonio. (1994). *Descarte's Error: Emotion, Reason, and the Human Brain*. New York: Penguin Books. Medical writer and founder of The Neuroscience Academy, Sarah Mckay Ph.D., refers to Damasio's distinction between emotions and feelings in her blog: http://yourbrainhealth.com.au, which is where I first read about the idea.

5   The School of Remembering. Accessed Nov. 15, 2016. http://theschoolofremembering.net/sor/

6   Aluna the Movie. Accessed Nov. 15, 2016. http://www.alunathemovie.com/

7   Reddy, Jini. "What Colombia's Kogi people can teach us about the environment." *The Guardian*, October 29, 2013. Accessed September

1, 2016. https://www.theguardian.com/sustainable-business/colombia-kogi-environment-destruction

8　Sedona Red Rock Tours website, in conjunction with the Coconino National Forest. Accessed December 7, 2016. http://www.sedonaredrocktours.com/sedona-spiritual-vortexes/

9　Image of Bell Rock in Sedona, Arizona from Scott McAllister Art Collections on Pinterest. Accessed September 1, 2016. https://www.pinterest.com/pin/419538521507988780/

10　Satsang with Mooji website. Accessed July 1, 2017. http://mooji.org/vaster-than-sky/#home

11　"Mooji's Biography." Satsang with Mooji website. Accessed July 1, 2016. https://mooji.org/biography/

12　The Desert Shaman website. Accessed July 1, 2017. http://www.thedesertshaman.com

13　Place, Robert. (1995). *The Alchemical Tarot*. London: Harper Collins.

14　Bunning, Joan. (1998). *Learning the Tarot: A Tarot Book for Beginners*. San Francisco, CA/Newburyport, MA: Weiser Books.

15　Pollack, Rachel. (2014). *The Burning Serpant Oracle: A Lenormand of the Soul*. Keysville, VA: Hermes Publications.

16　Driscoll, James F. (1911). "St. Raphael." In *The Catholic Encyclopedia*. New York: Robert Appleton Company. Accessed July 1, 2017. http://www.newadvent.org/cathen/12640b.htm

17　Crystal Wind is an information repository and portal for many spiritual and healing modalities on achieving or communicating effectively with and within the higher consciousness of self-realization. http://www.crystalwind.ca/moons-of-the-medicine-wheel/cornplanting-moon

18　Bear, Sun and Wind, Marlise Wabun. (1980). *The Medicine Wheel: Earth Astrology*. Touchstone. Kindle edition, 2011.

19　Yogananda, Paramhansa. (1998, 13th edition). *Autobiography of a Yogi*. Self-Realization Fellowship. Published in English, Bengali, Gujarati, Hindi, Kannada, Malayalam, Marathi, Oriya, Tamil, Telugu, Urdu, Japanese, Arabic, Greek, Icelandic, Danish, Dutch, Finnish, French, German, Italian, Nepali, polish, Purtuguese, Spanish, and Swedish. See pp. 411-428.

20 Ibid. p. 423-424.

21 Easwaran, Eknath. (1978). *Meditation: A Simple Eight-Point Program for Translating Spiritual Ideals into Daily Life*. Nilgiri Press. Translated into 14 languages, and later republished as *Passage Meditation: A Complete Spiritual Practice*. (2016).

22 Loyola Press. A Jesuit Ministry. (2017). "Peace Prayer of Saint Francis." Accessed July 1, 2017. http://www.loyolapress.com/our-catholic-faith/prayer/traditional-catholic-prayers/saints-prayers/peace-prayer-of-saint-francis

23 Easwaran, Eknath. (1987). *The Upanishads*. Tomales, CA: Nilgiri Press, p. 265.

24 Ibid.

25 Carter, Jimmy. (2009). "Losing my Religion for Equality." *The Age*, Jul. 14, 2009. Accessed March 1, 2017. http://www.theage.com.au/federal-politics/losing-my-religion-for-equality-20090714-dk0v.html?stb=fb

26 Yogananda, Paramhansa. (1998, 13th edition). *Autobiography of a Yogi*. Self-Realization Fellowship.

27 Carter, Jimmy. (2014). *A Call to Action: Women, Religion, Violence, and Power*. New York: Simon & Schuster.

28 Ibid, pp. 3-4.

29 Rinaldo, Rachel. "How a Growing Number of Muslim Women Clerics Are Challenging Traditional Narratives. *The Conversation*, June 6, 2017. Accessed July 11, 2017. https://theconversation.com/how-a-growing-number-of-muslim-women-clerics-are-challenging-traditional-narratives-77932

30 See: Hannagan, Charley. "Jerry Sandusky's son: How he groomed me to sexually abuse me." Central NY News. Syracuse.com, April 1, 2016. Accessed August 29, 2017. http://www.syracuse.com/news/index.ssf/2016/04/jerry_sanduskys_son_how_he_groomed_me_to_sexually_abuse_me.html; Ganim, Sara and Eric Levenson. "Jerry Sandusky's son facing child sex soliciting charges." CNN, February 14, 2017. Accessed August 30, 2017. http://www.cnn.com/2017/02/13/us/jerry-sandusky-son-charged/index.html

31 Miller, Alice. "'The Body Never Lies': A Challenge." July 1, 2005. Accessed April 1, 2017. https://www.alice-miller.com/en/the-body-never-lies-a-challenge/

32 Miller, Alice. (1981). *The Drama of the Gifted Child*. New York: Basic Books.

33 Excerpt from *Mein Kampf* by Adolf Hitler, edited by Dr. Richard Weikart, Stanislaus State University. This excerpt is the first section of Vol. 1, Chapter 11: Nation and Race. Accessed May 5, 2017. https://www.csustan.edu/history/mein-kampf

34 "Das Selbstporträt des Jürgen Bartsch (The Self-Portrait of Jürgen Bartsch)" appeared in 1972 [Frankfurt] and is currently out of print. An excerpt can be found here on Alice Miller's website: http://www.nospank.net/fyog15.htm

35 Kershaw, Ian. (2000, reprint ed.). *Hitler 1889 – 1936: Hubris*. New York/London: W.W. Norton & Company, pp. 12-13.

36 Miller, Alice (1991). *Breaking Down the Walls of Silence*. NY: Dutton/Penguin Books. Miller's critique of the commandment is expanded in her book *The Body Never Lies*.

37 Miller, Alice (1983). *For Your Own Good: Hidden Cruelty in Child-Rearing and the Roots of Violence*. New York: Farrar Straus Giroux.

38 U.S. Department of Veterans Affairs. National Center for PTSD. "How Common is PTSD?" Last updated October 3, 2016. 810 Vermont Avenue, NW Washington, DC 20420. Accessed July 1, 2017. https://www.ptsd.va.gov/public/ptsd-overview/basics/how-common-is-ptsd.asp

39 Duhigg, Charles. "Enemy Contact. Kill 'em, Kill 'em.'" *LA Times*, July 18, 2004. Accessed July 1, 2017. http://articles.latimes.com/2004/jul/18/world/fg-killing18

40 *Hazing in View: College Students at Risk* provides the initial findings of the National Study of Student Hazing. The research is based on the analysis of 11,482 survey responses from undergraduate students enrolled at 53 colleges and universities and more than 300 interviews with students and campus personnel at 18 of those institutions.

41 Hlavka, Heather. (2014). "Normalizing Sexual Violence: Young Women Account for Harassment and Abuse." *Gender & Society*, 28(3): 337-58.

[42] Gorman, Michele. "1 in 4 Women Experienced Sexual Assault While in College, Survey. Finds." *Newsweek*, September 21, 2015. Accessed July 11, 2017. http://www.newsweek.com/1-4-women-sexual-assault-college-374793

[43] Nettle, Neon. "Catholic Church: Women Are to Blame for Pedophile Priests." *Countercurrent News*, July 5, 2017. Accessed July 11, 2017. http://www.neonnettle.com/news/2359-catholic-church-women-are-to-blame-for-pedophile-priests

[44] Miller, Alice. (1996, Reissue Ed.). *Prisoners of Childhood: The Drama of the Gifted Child and the Search for the True Self.* New York: Basic Books, pp. 65-67.

[45] Felitti, V.J., Anda, R.F., Nordenberg, D., Williamson, D.F., Spitz, A., Edwards, V., Koss, M.P., Marks, J.S. (1998). "Relationship of Childhood and Household Dysfunction to Many of the Leading Causes of Death in Adults." *American Journal of Preventive Medicine*,14(4): 245-58. The large epidemiological study was a collaboration by researchers from the Centers for Disease Control and Prevention and Kaiser Permanente's Department of Preventive Medicine to examine the role of "adverse childhood experiences" (ACEs) on social and health outcomes later in life.

[46] Ibid.

[47] Miller, Alice. (1998). *Thou Shalt Not Be Aware: Society's Betrayal of the Child.* New York: Farrar Straus Giroux, pp: 7-8.

[48] Carter, Jimmy. (2014). *A Call to Action: Women, Religion, Violence, and Power.* New York: Simon & Schuster, p. 5.

[49] "Om Purnam." (2009). Recorded by Lakshmi, Jaya. On *Radiance*.

[50] Kripalu Center for Yoga & Health. (2017). "The Beginners' Guide to Kirtan and Mantra." Accessed May 1, 2017. https://kripalu.org/resources/beginners-guide-kirtan-and-mantra

[51] Brassard, Francis. (2000). *The Concept of Bodhicitta in Santideva's Bodhicaryavatara.* Albany, NY: State University of New York Press, p. 71.

[52] De Liso, Tom [a.k.a. Hermes Trismegistus]. (1995-2017.) "The Eleventh Chakra." In *The Pathwork Healing Series* on wisdomsdoor.com. Accessed July 1, 2017. https://www.wisdomsdoor.com/hb/hhb-24.php

53   Miller, Andrea. (2014). *Buddha's Daughters: Teachings from Women Who Are Shaping Buddhism in the West*. Boston, MA: Shambhala Publications, Inc.

54   Yogananda, Paramhansa. (1998, 13ᵗʰ edition). *Autobiography of a Yogi*. Self-Realization Fellowship. Published in English, Bengali, Gujarati, Hindi, Kannada, Malayalam, Marathi, Oriya, Tamil, Telugu, Urdu, Japanese, Arabic, Greek, Icelandic, Danish, Dutch, Finnish, French, German, Italian, Nepali, polish, Purtuguese, Spanish, and Swedish. See pp. 425.

55   Spencer, Neil. "Yoga Sutras 1.3: Tada Drashtuh Svarupe Avasthanam - Seer, Seeker & Seen are One." *Yoganonymous*, June 23, 2015. Accessed July 1, 2017. http://yoganonymous.com/yoga-sutra-1-3-tada-drashtuh-svarupe-avasthanam-seer-seeker-seen-are-one

56   Ibid.

57   Matson, John. "Fact or Fiction?: Lead Can Be Turned into Gold." *Scientific American*, January 31, 2014. Accessed July 1, 2017. https://www.scientificamerican.com/article/fact-or-fiction-lead-can-be-turned-into-gold/

58   Labyrinthos Academy. "The Severn Stages of Alchemical Transformation: A Spiritual Metaphor. (Infographic)." December 9, 2016. Accessed July 1, 2017. https://labyrinthos.co/blogs/learn-tarot-with-labyrinthos-academy/the-seven-stages-of-alchemical-transformation-a-spiritual-metaphor-infographic

59   Spira, Rupert. "Consciousness is Our True Body." *Youtube*, May 3, 2015. Accessed July 1, 2017. https://www.youtube.com/watch?v=VoU_bjtst7c

Printed in the United States
By Bookmasters